Sexual Crime

Sexual Crime is an edited book series devised by a team at SOCAMRU led by Professor Belinda Winder in the Psychology Division at Nottingham Trent University.

It offers original contributions to specific avenues of research within the field of sexual crime with each volume drawing together a review of the literature from across disciplines, including cutting edge research and practice, original material from services and offenders themselves as well as future directions for research and practice.

These volumes will be highly relevant to clinical and forensic psychologists and therapists, offender managers and supervisors, social workers and those working in the field of rehabilitation. They will be a great source of insight for academics, researchers and students in these disciplines as well as criminologists and policy makers.

Craig A. Harper · Rebecca Lievesley ·
Helen Swaby · Belinda Winder ·
Nicholas Blagden · Kerensa Hocken ·
Phil Banyard
Editors

Sexual Crime and the Internet

palgrave
macmillan

Editors
Craig A. Harper
Nottingham Trent University
Nottingham, UK

Rebecca Lievesley
Nottingham Trent University
Nottingham, UK

Helen Swaby
Nottingham Trent University
Nottingham, UK

Belinda Winder
Nottingham Trent University
Nottingham, UK

Nicholas Blagden
University of Derby
Derby, UK

Kerensa Hocken
His Majesty's Prison and Probation Service
Nottingham, UK

Phil Banyard
Nottingham Trent University
Nottingham, UK

ISSN 2628-8168 ISSN 2628-8176 (electronic)
Sexual Crime
ISBN 978-3-031-95843-4 ISBN 978-3-031-95844-1 (eBook)
https://doi.org/10.1007/978-3-031-95844-1

Cover credit: Connect Images/photoBertMyers

This Palgrave Macmillan imprint is published by the registered company Springer Nature Switzerland AG
The registered company address is: Gewerbestrasse 11, 6330 Cham, Switzerland

Preface

This Series: Sexual Crime

This book series will offer original contributions to current books available in this fast-growing area of high public interest. Each volume will comprehensively engage with current literature and make efforts to access unpublished literature and data by key authors in the field. The series will also, by the end of each volume, suggest potential new directions for researchers and practitioners.

These volumes are relevant not just to psychologists, criminologists, social workers, final year undergraduate, postgraduate, doctoral students of all these areas but to practitioners and the general public with an interest in learning more about the topic. The aim is to create books that are readable, yet firmly anchored in a sound evidence base from both researchers and practitioners. The volumes will include therefore a robust synthesis of the literature, consideration of the theories relevant to each topic, a focus on projects that are relevant to the topic, with a summary of the research and evaluation of these, chapters focusing on the service user voice and a final summary chapter, highlighting future possibilities and directions (as suggested by others in the field or by the authors themselves).

This Volume: Sexual Crime and the Internet

The volume begins with an exploration of the theoretical underpinnings of the effect of the internet on the development of sexual deviance, before looking at more applied topics including online sexual offending against children and sextortion. Contemporary topics such as image-based sexual abuse, dating app-facilitated violence, and groups referred to as 'incels' are also explored.

Nottingham, UK	Craig A. Harper
Nottingham, UK	Rebecca Lievesley
Nottingham, UK	Helen Swaby
Nottingham, UK	Belinda Winder
Derby, UK	Nicholas Blagden
Nottingham, UK	Kerensa Hocken
Nottingham, UK	Phil Banyard

Contents

Editors and Contributors

About the Editors

Craig Harper is an Associate Professor in Psychology at Nottingham Trent University. His research interests lie in the psychological processes that underpin decision-making in relation to controversial social and political topics. Most of his research has been focused on how people form and express attitudes towards people with sexual convictions, with the aim being to promote progressive and evidence-based policies to prevent and reduce sexual victimisation. Away from forensically-based research, he is a member of the Heterodox Academy, which is an organisation seeking to promote viewpoint diversity and reduce political polarisation in higher education.

Rebecca Lievesley is an Associate Professor in Psychology at Nottingham Trent University. She has been conducting research within the criminal justice system since 2008, including an investigation of reoffending and desistance in those serving short sentences, and the evaluation of the use of medication to manage problematic sexual arousal for individuals convicted of a sexual offence. Her current research focus relates to the prevention of sexual offending among, and effective treatment of, non-offending populations with self-identified paedophilia.

Belinda Winder is Professor of Forensic Psychology and Research Director for the Centre of Crime, Offending, Prevention and Engagement (COPE) at Nottingham Trent University. Working with people with lived experience, she seeks to make a difference in the world by designing and undertaking mixed-method research to inform and provide evidence-based practice and policy. Her primary field is sexual offending, but she also has a particular interest in life after prison and the (re)integration of people with criminal records into the community.

Contributors

Ian Baker is a survivor of two police forces and three universities in the UK who is now reflecting on those events in a more sedate life. Having investigated the grimier aspects of life he went on to research some, with a particular focus on victim and perpetrators' experiences.

Nicholas Blagden is a Professor of Criminological Psychology. He is a Chartered Psychologist and has worked and researched within the criminal justice system and HM Prison Service for many years.

Phil Banyard is an Emeritus Professor in Psychology at Nottingham Trent University, UK. He has previously been honoured with the British Psychological Society's Award for Distinguished Contributions to Psychology Education.

William Costello is a Ph.D. student of Individual Differences and Evolutionary Psychology at the University of Texas at Austin. In 2021, William graduated with an M.Sc. in Psychology, Culture and Evolution from Brunel University London. He is the American Psychological Association Division 51 Society for the Psychological Study of Men and Masculinities Student of the Year for 2023. His work has been published in journals such as *Evolutionary Psychological Science and the Journal of Sex Research*. In 2024, William and his colleagues from Swansea University (Drs. Andrew Thomas and Joe Whittaker) conducted the largest piece of incel research on behalf of the UK Government's Commission for Countering Extremism (CCE).

Rosa Dreyhaupt obtained her Bachelor's degree in Psychology (B.Sc.) and her Master's degree in Forensic Psychology (M.Sc.) from Maastricht University. Through her work in a prison and a forensic psychiatric facility in Brandenburg, Germany, as well as her collaboration with research teams in the UK and Sweden, she gained experience in both practice and research on the topic of child sexual offending. She is set to complete her training as a cognitive behavioural psychotherapist in the fall of 2025 at the Deutsche Gesellschaft für Verhaltenstherapie (DGVT).

Simon Duff 0is an Associate Professor at the University of Nottingham, England where he is the Director of Stage II Training in Forensic Psychology. In addition to his academic role, he provides individual intervention at an NHS low-secure forensic service. Simon's research interests lie in the areas of stalking, sexual offending, and the effects of pornography.

Harriet Dymond is an Assistant Professor at the University of Nottingham, England. Aside from academia, Harriet works within the Safer Living Foundation; a Nottingham-based charity aimed at supporting those convicted of, or in fear of committing, sexually offensive behaviour. Harriet has particular expertise in the field of preventing sexual offending against children, leading community-based therapeutic initiatives for minor-attracted people with no prior criminal histories.

Dean Fido is an Associate Professor of Forensic Psychology based at the University of Derby (UK). His expertise lies within the field of image-based sexual abuse; specifically, the role of dark and deviant personality traits and behaviours which facilitate offending behaviour. Dr. Fido also consults on technology-facilitated violence and violence against women and girls more broadly and is co-chair of the European branch of the Aftermath Foundation, which produces educational materials for victims of domestic abuse.

Rebecca Fisico, M.Sc., is a Clinical Psychology Ph.D. student at McMaster University. She received her B.A. (Hons) and M.Sc. in Forensic Psychology from Ontario Tech University. Her current primary research interest is studying technology-facilitated sexual violence, with a particular focus on exploring the factors associated with adults engaging in these behaviours.

Kerensa Hocken is a registered forensic psychologist with oversight for the assessment and treatment of people in prison for sexual offending in the Midlands region.

Daria Kuss is a Chartered Psychologist, Chartered Scientist, and Associate Professor in Psychology at Nottingham Trent University. Her research concerns the psychological aspects of Internet and technology use. She is specifically interested in understanding the place of technology use in today's technophilic culture, including the benefits and drawbacks of different types of technology use.

Derek Perkins is a Clinical & Forensic Psychologist, Visiting Professor of Forensic Psychology at Royal Holloway University of London and Co-Director of the onlineProtect research group. For over 20 years, he was Head of Psychological Services at Broadmoor High Security Psychiatric Hospital, having previously worked in the UK Prison Service and Midland Centre for Forensic Psychiatry. He has specialised in assessment and interventions for sexual offending, including child sexual abuse, internet-related sexual offending, and sexual homicide.

Brandon Sparks, Ph.D., FHEA is a Postdoctoral Fellow at the University of New Brunswick investigation police responses to intimate partner violence cases. He received his M.A. and Ph.D. from the University of Saskatchewan. His research interests span the nexus between healthy and unhealthy relationships with an emphasis on sexual violence, particularly technology-facilitated sexual violence. He has also published research exploring the psychosocial issues experienced by members of the involuntary celibacy (incel) community.

Helen Swaby is a Senior Lecturer in Counselling and Psychological Therapies at Nottingham Trent University, UK. She has a background in forensic psychology and integrative psychotherapy.

Tadgh Tobin is currently completing his Ph.D. at Nottingham Trent University, exploring how individuals conceptualise non-consensual penetrative sex, and the implications of variance within these concepts. Tadgh has formerly completed a B.Sc. in Psychology at Nottingham Trent University and an M.Sc. in Forensic Psychology at Manchester Metropolitan University, completing research projects in predicting rape proclivity and rape victim empathy, respectively.

Sarah Wefers is a Practitioner-Researcher with Stop It Now UK & Ireland and the Lucy Faithfull Foundation. She has over 10 years of experience in conducting research in the area of online and contact child sexual offending and working with people who have engaged in, or are at risk of, sexual offending against children. This included working at Prevention Project Dunkelfeld in Germany, and several research positions, collaborating with law enforcement and non-governmental organisations.

List of Figures

List of Tables

CHAPTER 1

The Internet and Sexual Arousal: Development, Maintenance, and Escalation of Sexual Offending

Simon C. Duff and Harriet Dymond

Introduction

The internet is an expanding[1] collection of connected hardware systems, software, information, and activity, providing an environment for human endeavour, embedded within cultures (Miller & Slater, 2000; Ponzanesi, 2020). As it is an element of culture (Foley, 2020), it is valuable to explore how the internet may impact behaviour. Evidence shows that it does have

[1] At 10:10 in the morning of 6 June 2020, it was estimated that there were over 4.5 billion internet users in the world, with the number rising by approximately 7 users every second that this chapter outline was written, which approximates to 58% of the global population. At the same time, there were approximately 1.7 billion websites, increasing at a rate of two per second (https://www.internetlivestats.com/).

S. C. Duff (✉)
University of Nottingham, Nottingham, UK
e-mail: simon.duff@nottingham.ac.uk

H. Dymond
Keele University, Staffordshire, UK

C. A. Harper et al. (eds.), *Sexual Crime and the Internet*, Sexual Crime,
https://doi.org/10.1007/978-3-031-95844-1_1

impact, both negative and positive, on several aspects of our lives; research concerned with the relationship between internet use and emotion has shown that greater use is associated with loneliness (Moretta & Buodo, 2020) and depression (Banjanin et al., 2015). Conversely, the Pew Internet Project (2000), part of a larger research study concerned with issues and trends that have an impact globally, found that the internet allowed women to feel more emotionally supported within their established relationships. Nonetheless, it has also been claimed that the internet can act to facilitate offending (Stalans & Finn, 2016). The word 'can' is crucial here, as the internet is often presented as an open tap pouring its content into our uncontrolled, ever-hungry minds. However, except where there are genuine issues of addiction (which itself is complex, see Hogarth, 2020) the reality is that we choose what we search for, consume, and allow into our lives. For example, the tabloid newspaper *The Sun* is difficult to buy in print form in Liverpool,[2] but it is available online; Liverpool football fans are not forcibly exposed to it just because it is available on the internet.

This chapter is concerned with exploring the impact of the internet on one aspect of human behaviour, sexual offending. It is important to note that the focus here is on criminal behaviour rather than simply risky sexual behaviour as the two are quite different. It has been established that exposure to sexually explicit materials can play a role in decreasing, for example, empathy (Allen et al., 1995) and increasing sexually permissive attitudes and behaviour in young people (Lo & Wei, 2005), but these are not necessarily directly linked to offending. As Barnett and Mann (2013a) stated, the evidence base for empathy and sexual offending is weak and inconsistent and Righthand and Welch (2004) state regarding youths who have offended sexually and their sexually permissive behaviour, 'Research also suggests that *sometimes* their experiences have exceeded the experience of control juveniles who have not committed sex offenses' (p22—emphasis added). We seek to examine how internet use may form a part of the development, maintenance, and escalation of sexual offending.

[2] This is a result of its coverage of the 1989 Hillsborough disaster, which portrayed Liverpool football fans in an extremely negative light, suggesting that they 'pickpocketed the dead and urinated on police' (see https://www.bbc.co.uk/news/uk-england-merseyside-17113382). While there is no de facto ban on the sale of *The Sun* in Liverpool, it is still very hard to come by.

There are several reasons that the internet may play a role in sexual offending. Pornography makes up a large proportion of the information available on the internet, and it is estimated that approximately 12% of all websites are pornographic (Ahmed et al., 2016). It is also easily accessible, which is one of the three factors that Cooper et al. (2004) identified as important pulls towards internet use. They refer to these as the 'Triple-A Engine': Anonymity, Accessibility, and Affordability.

Here, we consider three crucial questions:

1. Does the internet increase the likelihood of exposure to sexually explicit material?
2. Does the internet increase the likelihood of exposure to a greater breadth of sexually explicit material, from softcore to hardcore?
3. Does the sexually explicit material that is accessible through the internet—be it images, text, video, or audio—differentially impact on how we respond to it and how it affects us?

Each of these considerations is important when discussing sexual offending, and similar questions were posed by Bauserman (1996) over a quarter of a century ago. The fact that this debate continues provides some indication of the complexity of trying to be definitive in this area. It is also useful to be aware that there is no internationally recognised definition of pornography, no international consensus on law, and that both what counts as pornography and where it lies on the soft–hard continuum is subjective, regardless of scientific definitions or legal rulings.

Before we focus on pornography, there is an important caveat to keep in mind when we think about its use, perhaps particularly when considering its more extreme forms. This is the question of what else has been occurring in an individual's life that might independently impact upon pornographic use and offending. For example, it is plausible that early experiences may impact both on an individual's use of pornography and their likelihood of offending, independently, as predicted by the revised version of Ward and Beech's (2016) integrated theory of sexual offending. Their theory provides examples of childhood experiences that have been associated with offending behaviour such as exposure to sexual stimuli and additionally they identify that sexualised behaviour, such as compulsive masturbation, may lead to offending, which may be a drive to seek pornography as a stimulus. Thus, caution is required when considering that exposure to pornography is producing deviant behaviour, when seeking pornography may be a resultant behaviour of a pre-existing deviance.

Exposure and Consumption

For clarity, it should be noted that, within this chapter, we consider 'consumption' to be based on a *decision* to interact with pornography, whereas 'exposure' is the *inadvertent* viewing of pornography. We do, however, recognise that the terms are frequently used interchangeably. The first things we might reasonably ask are, 'Does the internet increase the exposure to and consumption of pornography'? and 'Is the kind of pornography that is available changing?'. These are not simple questions to answer, as pre-internet statistics relating to pornography consumption are hindered by the underground nature of the pornography industry at that time. Furthermore, the fact that a paper copy of *Penthouse* was purchased does not tell us how many people may have seen it, as is true for the sale of a video tape of *Debbie Does Dallas* (https://en.wikipedia.org/wiki/Debbie_Does_Dallas). It is also important to note that over the past five decades, each revolution in communication (e.g., the video cassette recorder) has resulted in warnings of likely increased exposure to pornography (see: Bonniwell, 1971; Brosius et al., 1993). This perspective would also lead to the assumption that the advent of the internet would have resulted in increases in exposure and consumption.

Have Exposure and Consumption Increased?

When we examine the statistics, we find that in 2012 it was estimated that 10% of the material available on the internet was pornography (Ogas & Gaddam, 2012). Cronin (2008) estimated that between 10,000 and 15,000 pornographic films are produced in the US annually. In 2006, estimates suggested that every second, there were 28,258 people viewing pornography on the internet (Joyce, 2008). However, the evidence for large increases in exposure and consumption is absent. Wright (2013) estimated that from the early 1970s to the mid-1980s pornography consumption by males in the US increased by 0.03% annually, and that from 1986 to 2010 this increase was 0.01%. In a similar study that took into consideration the age of both men and women in cohorts from 1973 to 2012, Price et al. (2016) suggested that pornography consumption increased: by 16.1% in males of all ages, and 4.4% in females (for both genders, the greatest increases were for the 27–35 age group: 21.9% for males and 10.2% for females). Thus, despite the internet providing an apparently ever-increasing amount of pornography—a 28-fold increase in dedicated webpages from 1999 to 2007—there has not been a corresponding increase in consumption and exposure in adults. Naturally, this does not mean that pornography on the internet is unproblematic; however, the problem does not appear to be based predominantly on an increase in the number of people being exposed to or consuming pornography.

For young people, the issue of pornographic exposure and consumption rates is as complex. In Lo and Wei's (2005) study of 2,001 high-school students in Taiwan, 37.9% reported that they had been exposed to internet pornography, and 37.7% reported that they had been exposed to pornographic comics; thus, at that time, the internet was providing no greater access than a print medium. In a similar US-based study, Ybarra and Mitchell (2005) reported that 8% of their sample of 1,501 10–17-year-olds described actively seeking online pornography. Over the last 15 years, however, the picture has changed. Figures for people aged 14–17 purposefully consuming pornography on a regular basis have increased, ranging from 19 and 30% of boys and girls across five European countries, including England (Stanley et al., 2018). Furthermore, a report written by the NSPCC suggests that anywhere between 4 and 32% of 10–18-year-olds have viewed illegal pornography of some kind (Hollis & Belton, 2017).

The fact that the internet supports earlier access to pornography is crucial to understanding the risk of offending behaviour. People with an earlier age of onset of accessing adult pornography have shown an increased likelihood of later accessing indecent images of children or bestiality material (Seigfried-Spellar & Rogers, 2013). However, such studies have not examined the potential implication of arousal in this process. While attention needs to be paid to distinguishing accidental exposure from purposeful consumption, for young people in particular, the internet has provided a medium through which they can easily and anonymously access pornographic content at a higher rate. Removing sexual arousal from the equation for the time being, for children and young people, the internet provides an almost surplus supply of 'answers' and information about sex, sexuality, and sexual behaviour, some or all of which may be absent or insufficiently addressed in school environments (Rothman et al., 2015; Ybarra et al., 2014). It is thus plausible that some of the increase in pornography access by young people is for more intellectual purposes rather than for sexual gratification alone, a position put forward by Tsaliki (2015).

Types of Pornography

When considering the potential impact of pornography, it is important to take into account the range of material that commonly is referred to as pornographic. We will all have our own views, and these views are undoubtedly influenced by our gender, age, experiences, beliefs, and countless other aspects that contribute to how we form opinions. If we consider that pornography lies on a continuum it is likely that the lower end of that scale there will be more disagreement, than at the higher end that involves sexual violence, humiliation, and uncommon sexual practices yet, as Rea (2001) argues, a clear definition of what constitutes pornography. 'is as elusive as the referent is pervasive' (p. 118). However, the history of research concerned with pornography has suggested that it is the more violent forms of pornography that result in negative effects, such as sexual aggression (e.g., Vega & Malamuth, 2007) and as such we might be particularly concerned with understanding the use of these more extreme forms of pornography.

The extent to which people access extreme pornography is hard to be measure, as there will be avenues to find extremes of pornography that require access to the dark web and private sharing between individuals (although the dark web is not quite the digital Wild West, as it is often portrayed; see Gehl (2016)). However, one view of pornography is that it is gradually becoming more extreme over time, and that individuals seek out more extreme pornography the more they engage with it; this is known as the 'content-progression thesis' (Landripet et al., 2019). Research that has examined mainstream online pornography suggests that heterosexual pornography is not becoming more violent in general and that which is violent is less frequently accessed (Shor & Seida, 2019). A recent study of adolescents found there was not a positive association between the amount of pornography that they consumed and the extremeness of that pornography; furthermore, over time, the degree of extreme pornography was found to decrease (Landripet et al., 2019). Evidence also suggests that only some people have an interest in violent or sexually violent pornography. For example, Demaré et al. (1988) found in their sample of 205 undergraduate males that 81% reported they used non-violent pornography, whereas 41% used violent pornography and 35% sexually violent pornography.

What Can Explain These Trends?
There may be several good reasons for the data suggesting only a small increase in consumption and exposure. Firstly, consumption figures are mostly based on the US, and they may not reflect global changes in areas where pre-internet data are not available: pre-internet pornography made in the UK was unlikely to surface in India, but the internet provides fast and cheap international access. Secondly, census data are often based on simplistic questions regarding pornography, such as 'Have you ever watched an X-rated movie?'. The concept of an 'X-rated movie' is not widely in use now, and it does not reflect the wealth of ways in which pornography is presented online. Issues with research also arguably affect the extent to which we can clearly understand the role of pornography in sexual offending; the majority of such data are based on self-reports, involving asking people who have committed sexual offences to think about their pornography use retrospectively or asking pornography users (who may or may not go on to offend sexually) to respond to questionnaires about their present, or hypothetical, selves. With regard to why the more violent pornography may not be increasing in popularity, it is possible that as pornography is aimed at sexual arousal, the majority of individuals do not find sexual violence arousing, and if attempts are made to incorporate it into sexual behaviour with partners this may receive a negative response from those sexual partners. Finally, although the internet is widely available, it is also possible to prevent access to certain materials. For example, in the location at which the present author (SD) is now writing, there are systems in place to prevent access to pornography. Ybarra and Mitchell (2005) state that 27% of the caregivers to the children in their study reported that they had installed software to block pornography on their computers. Therefore, while we might view the internet as the Id, it is possible to have a Superego in place to manage us if we cannot manage ourselves.

Our best estimate of the effect of the internet in relation to pornography is that it has increased consumption and exposure, but that those increases are not as dramatic as we might have assumed, despite the greater availability of pornographic material, and that the type of pornography that is considered most problematic is less preferred and less accessed.

Arousal

Arousal typically refers to a state of alertness to stimuli and is considered to be central to motivating basic behaviours such as seeking food, avoiding fights, and accessing sex. Although this definition holds true when focussing on sexual stimuli, it tends to have the additional meaning of responding sexually to sexual stimuli, either physiologically, psychologically, or both. Studies that focus on arousal to sexual stimuli frequently simply ask participants to provide a rating for the question, 'How sexually arousing do you find this stimulus?' (e.g., Laier et al., 2013—the authors do not define what they mean by sexually arousing), or may measure physiological changes through plethysmography (e.g., Wouda et al., 1998). As studies have shown that there can be a disconnect between psychological ratings and physiological responses of arousal (Rupp & Wallen, 2008), it is suggested that arousal may not be suitably understood. In this chapter, we consider that arousal will relate to both physiological and psychological consequences.

Sexual Arousal and Criminal Behaviour

Why might sexual arousal be an issue of focus when considering criminal behaviour? Based on work with Japanese dancing mice, Yerkes and Dodson (1908) suggested that physiological arousal can improve task performance up to a certain point, after which it inhibits it. Easterbrook (1959) proposed that this might be due to the limiting effect that arousal has on attention to information; that is, we use less information to make decisions when we are aroused beyond a certain limit. Regardless of whether we view criminal behaviour as a product of poor decision-making from a state or a trait perspective, these very early views of the effects of arousal raise the possibility that, for some people, some stimuli may be arousing enough that they can impact upon cognition, and cognition plays a role in behaviour. Certainly, we might imagine that while one is aroused, one's decision-making can change; this is an argument that has been used to explain why people describe sex as pleasurable when they will also describe sex-related stimuli out of context (e.g., saliva, semen, body odour) as disgusting (see Borg & de Jong, 2012). Similarly, Van den Bergh et al. (2008) describe a phenomenon they have named 'The Bikini Effect', in which sexual arousal reduces human capacity for empathy and increases impulsive proclivities and risky, thrill-seeking behaviours, all of which may be implicated in the development, maintenance, and escalation of sexual offending (Barnett & Mann, 2013b; Efrati et al., 2019). However, are there longer-lasting effects of arousal—either on current or future cognition—that might help us understand the potential link between arousal and offending?

From a simple behavioural perspective, arousal can be viewed as a reward, and if one becomes aroused to pornography (which is at least part of what makes something pornographic), then it is plausible that one will continue to seek out more pornography (Hald et al., 2014). However, viewing pornography is not necessarily illegal, and any links between pornography and criminal behaviour are mere associations that may not be linked to arousal per se. This has been demonstrated in countries where pornography was prohibited then permitted (allowing researchers to accurately monitor behavioural and societal changes; see Diamond et al., 2011), in which associations have not been found between the availability of pornography and the rates of sexual crime.

Peter and Valkenburg (2008) carried out a study in adolescents demonstrating that sexually explicit internet material (SEIM) increased sexual preoccupation, with this relationship fully mediated by arousal. However, they did not track any changes in the content of the SEIM that was accessed during the year of the study, so there is no evidence of escalation in the nature of the material towards illegality. Studies with people who have committed offences suggest that easy and frequent exposure to SEIM can result in reduced arousal to that material, resulting in curiosity and then a genuine interest in more extreme sexual material (Rimer, 2016), along with further desensitisation, depersonalisation (De Almeida Neto et al., 2011), and disinhibition (Suler, 2004). Thus, it is possible that the internet could increase the risk of accessing illegal material in vulnerable populations, i.e., those who have offended, through a process of 'chasing arousal'. This mirrors findings with other forms of behaviour that can become problematic, such as gambling, where research has shown that the possibility of winning money results in heightened physiological arousal, and those positive feelings may diminish over time, leading the gambler to seek arousal through taking larger risks (see Wulfert et al., 2005).

Is Arousal to Internet Pornography Different?

Brand et al. (2011) demonstrated that subjectively rated arousal to pornographic pictures on the internet, as provided by 89 heterosexual males, partly predicts self-reported issues of excessive internet use related to sexual activity. Thus, the extent to which one further engages with internet pornography—and any risk that might raise—can be increased by arousal to online sexual material. A follow-up study by Laier et al., (2013) supported these findings in a sample of 171 heterosexual males. In addition, they compared 25 males described as 'healthy' users with 25 self-identified 'problematic' users and found that the problematic users experienced greater arousal to the same stimuli. They conclude that this is not an effect of a poor sexual life, but rather it is due to the positive reinforcement (via masturbation) that results. These findings suggest that sexual arousal to online material can impact on further online sexual activity, although the authors do not explore what their ratings of sexual arousal refer to, for example, if the participants were rating their physiological arousal to the images.

We might hypothesise that this relationship between arousal to images and problematic internet use has the potential to lead to online offending, and thus that arousal to online pornography is somehow exclusive to further online behaviour. Some findings from Laier et al. (2014) raise concerns with this hypothesis. They have demonstrated that high levels of arousal impact upon decision-making in gambling tasks, both because arousal leads to decisions to maximise further exposure and because it negatively influences the ability to learn where the choice of sexual stimulus leads to gambling losses. Therefore, sexual material can both be distracting—which we might expect—and make learning less successful. The crucial question is whether these effects of sexual arousal extend to situations distanced in time and place from the initial sexual exposure.

Evidence does suggest that online pornography has a longer-term impact on working memory, and this has been found to extend to situations away from the computer (see Young, 2008). Later research also indicated that exposure to pornography can impact upon non-conscious processes (Kunaharan et al., 2017), so it is plausible that there may be longer-term, more complex interactions between exposure to pornography and cognition. However, there does not appear to be research that specifically examines whether the medium of accessing pornography has a specific impact and thus whether the simple fact that it is available on the internet is somehow related to a greater risk of sexual offending. It may well be that the issues lie with consequential factors such as greater ease of availability and greater issues with managing what is available.

Exposure to Internet Pornography and Offending

Ideally, to specifically answer the question of the impact of the internet on sexual offending, we would have studies comparing internet users of pornography with those who use pornography away from the internet, with a control group who have not been exposed to pornography. However, there are a variety of issues with such studies. Internet vs non-internet pornography consumption is likely to also include generational or societal differences that may exert a larger effect than the differences in how pornography is accessed. To find a control group who have not been exposed to pornography will likely raise the same issues. Importantly, we would need to consider whether it was possible to find people who (a) are representative of the general public, and (b) have not been exposed to pornography at any level, including through advertising, television, or film. To date, we have found no examples of such studies; as such, we must rely on work that has examined the impact of the internet on sexual offending and the impact of pornography on sexual offending.

Kendall (2006) suggested that US data from the period 1998–2003 show that the introduction of the internet (and thus easier access to pornography) was associated with reduced incidents of rape, but not other crimes, leading him to suggest that pornography could be construed as a substitute for rape. Similarly, using German data, Nolte (2017) found that access to the internet had no impact on rape but was associated with a reduction in child sex abuse. This finding is in line with research by Quayle and Taylor (2002), who interviewed men who were accessing sexual images of children. One stated, 'I didn't feel the urge as strongly as I do now to try and start something with a child ... when I was on-line with the child porn ... because when I felt that urge I'd look at the child porn' (p. 339).

Diegmann (2019) found similar results in relation to increased internet speed. He suggested that increased internet speeds may lead to a displacement of behaviour: the easy availability of more extreme pornography leads to fewer contact crimes taking place. However, he also notes that a reduced rate of offences in Germany may be offset by more offences (relating to sexualised images of children) in other countries, as the extreme materials must be produced somewhere. These results suggest either that pornography may be a protective factor generally or, as Diegmann suggests, it might act as a local protective factor, with the risk increasing in places where illegal images and films are produced. However, Norwegian data analysed by Bhuller et al. (2013) suggest that there is a link between access to broadband internet (and thus pornography) and rape. These findings mirror those of the impact of pornography on offending, whereby some studies suggest that there is an association (Donnerstein et al., 1987; Marshall et al., 1988) and others suggest that there is not (Kimmel & Linders, 1996; Winick & Evans, 1996).

In many studies that do demonstrate an association between pornography consumption and offending behaviour, it is not possible to identify the contribution of the internet. For example, Rostad et al. (2019) showed an association between pornography consumption and teenage dating violence in both boys and girls; however, their measure for pornography consumption asked about videos, magazines, films, or books, and it did not attempt to differentiate between videos and films from different sources. We thus have studies that could potentially throw light on this area, but they have generally taken a very broad approach to the consumption of pornography.

Importantly, when considering this kind of research, we need to keep in mind inconsistencies in the way in which pornography is conceptualised. In the UK, we use terms such as 'soft-core' and 'hard-core' to describe the level of explicitness of the sex depicted. There are also other dimensions to consider, such as the level of violence or coercion involved, if adults are depicted, whether the acts and participants involved are considered to be homosexual or heterosexual, or whether the material involves consensual pain, children, animals, or a whole variety of other factors. As the range of available pornography is vast, it is impossible to be conclusive about the effects of pornography more generally.

Development of Offending Behaviour

When contemplating the role of the internet in developing deviance, it is vital to consider individual differences. Internet pornography is a form of media, and the relationship between certain personality traits and the motivations to seek—and responses to—certain media content have been well established (see Bryant, 2009). This association has been conceptualised within a framework known as the 'uses and gratifications perspective' (Bryant, 2009; Finn, 1997; Rubin, 1994), whereby media usage gratifies a certain need in an individual. Researchers have studied whether the same applies to pornography and arousal. Understanding the need that pornography may meet in an individual, and the physiological or behavioural responses an individual may have to that content, are important aspects to consider when thinking about sexual deviance, as not all those exposed to the same pornography will be equally aroused, nor will they all adopt potentially sexually criminal attitudes or behaviour.

Bryant (2009) aimed to investigate the role of four variables on different types of pornography consumption and subsequent arousal: gender, sensation seeking, antisocial traits (specifically psychopathy), and dispositional sexual affect (enduring traits that dictate how a person responds and behaves towards sexually themed content and situations). Generally, men consumed and reported more arousal to online pornography than women, and the strongest predictor of arousal across both genders was dispositional sexual affect, but only in response to what Bryant's participants named 'standard fare' pornographic content. Arousal to content of a nonstandard, specialised nature for males was correlated with the disinhibition dimension of sensation seeking, and the interpersonal manipulation, antisocial, and impulsive thrill-seeking elements of psychopathy. For women, arousal to specialised content was weakly associated with only the antisocial behaviour element of psychopathy. The results of this study suggest that individual personality needs act as drivers for using certain pornography instead of necessarily meeting one's sexual needs. Interestingly, the antisocial aspect of personality seems to be associated with more extreme or non-standard forms of pornography, leaving the conundrum of which drives which: does pornography exposure increase one's antisocial traits, or do antisocial traits drive one towards more extreme forms of pornography? This is important to disentangle because we need to understand whether pornography is generally risky or if it is only risky to those who are vulnerable to it.

As is the case for non-sexual crime, individual differences pertain to risk factors, which are fundamental in understanding the function, nature, and prevention of deviant behaviour (Tanner-Smith et al., 2013). Hald and Malamuth (2015) exposed 200 males and females in Denmark to (non-violent) pornography under experimental conditions and investigated the effect of this exposure, past pornography consumption, and the Five Factor Model trait of agreeableness (Costa & McCrae, 1992) on attitudes consistent with violence towards women. They found certain trends in those expressing higher levels of attitudes supportive of violence towards women following exposure: they were lower in the agreeableness trait and had higher figures of past pornography consumption, and this was seen across males and females. For males specifically, agreeableness acted as a *moderator* between the experimental pornography exposure and such attitudes, and in men that were particularly low in agreeableness, it was found that arousal acted as a *mediator* in this relationship. While the outcomes measured in this study were taken soon after pornography exposure (as opposed to a longer-term measurement), the researchers demonstrated how pornographic content implicates attitudes and cognitions identified as risk factors for sexual offending (Seto et al., 2001) and highlighted how any possible relationship between pornography and sexual deviance cannot be described as a simple cause-and-effect mechanism without examining the functions of individual dispositions, past pornography consumption, and arousal.

Various models and theoretical frameworks have been designed to guide our understanding of pornography and its effects. However, each of these offers a different perspective on how individual personality variance is implicated in arousal and, potentially, antisocial attitudes. Individual influences on sexual aggression are heavily implicated in the hierarchical confluence model (HCM), which acted as the guiding theoretical background for Hald and Malamuth's (2015) work. The HCM considers how pornographic content affects a person's sexually aggressive proclivity only in relation to their individual risk and personality factors (Hald & Malamuth, 2015; Hald et al., 2014; Vega & Malamuth, 2007). Therefore, although pornography is designed to generate arousal, an individual's risk of deviance will fluctuate due to their *pre-existing* personality traits, attitudes, and cognitions (Hald & Malamuth, 2015). Mosher's sexual involvement theory (SIT; Mosher, 1988) also substantiates the importance of a person's individual predilections when considering arousal, predicting that an individual's engagement with pornography is inseparably associated with their own subjective sexual scripts. When considering pornography and the development of sexual deviance, these models suggest that the key feature of any association is each person's individual disposition, attitudes, and traits that are consistent with sexual offending. What is less clear is whether pornography can moderate dispositions, attitudes, and sexual scripts, for example in ways that impact on particular proclivities.

Agreeableness and psychopathy have been cited in the literature in relation to pornography, arousal, and sexual deviance due to these traits' influence on a person committing interpersonally exploitative, manipulative, or combative behaviour (Hare, 1982; Jensen-Campbell & Graziano, 2001), and for psychopathy in particular, the association with other antisocial media activities Williams (2002) identified psychopathy traits to be positively correlated with the consumption of more violent films, video games, and sports. Studies have demonstrated an association between arousal and these traits, but what is interesting to consider is the direction and influence of this relationship. Bryant (2009) identified certain psychopathic traits that predict consumption and arousal to certain pornographic categories; however, it is unclear whether this relationship is entirely unidirectional or whether pornography can in return influence our individual nature and tendency to offend. Williams et al. (2009) investigated the role of individual differences in determining whether sexually deviant fantasies become sexually deviant behaviours in non-offending samples, and they identified definitive correlations between sexual fantasies and behavioural tendencies, also finding that pornography consumption was positively associated with more frequent deviancy. However, as the authors identified, it is impossible to identify the exact direction and nature of this association. It is still of importance to consider the direction of the relationship between pornography and offending behaviour and the role of individual differences: is it the presence of these personality elements that drives an individual's desire to seek out pornography, become aroused, and potentially offend, or is it the pornography itself that influences the degree to which the person experiences these certain relevant personality variants and associated arousal, both of which may be implicated in offending?

So far, we have considered whether there might be a directly sexual impact of pornography, but it would be remiss to not consider another element: the ways in which pornography presents its actors, and the impacts that this might have. If we consider *Debbie Does Dallas* as an example, the male characters are portrayed as preoccupied and driven by sex; the females are not, but they are compliant and prepared to engage in any kind of sexual activity, anywhere, whether with or without some kind of gain. This cliché, whereby females are presented as eventually persuaded to engage in sex despite any initial protestations, is a repeated trope in mainstream pornography, whether online or otherwise, as it has been in mainstream media that was not predominantly pornographic, for example the early Bond films. Is it plausible that this could result in attitudes about sex and females that could develop into sexual offending? Hald et al. (2013) demonstrated that for individuals low in agreeableness, exposure to pornography increases sexist attitudes to females when individuals were more aroused by that pornography. They also showed that in males, increased levels of reported past pornography use were associated with more negative attitudes. This suggests that both historical and current pornography use can impact how males think about females—in the former, across males, and in the latter, in males with lower levels of agreeableness, suggesting different mechanisms for the development of negative attitudes and different vulnerabilities. More recently, female-perpetrated sexual aggression has been examined within a model of personality and pornography use; it was found that histrionic and narcissistic traits were predictive of several forms of sexually coercive behaviour (Hughes et al., 2020).

Maintenance

After psychological and physical arousal to a certain stimulus has developed, this arousal can be easily reinforced using the internet through frequent stimulus exposure and concurrent masturbation or sexual gratification (Burton et al., 2002), which can escalate in severity for some online users (as discussed later in this chapter). Sexual deviancy may be easily maintained within the confines of the computer, ostensibly because of the distance the user perceives from their actions and their consequences. As Carnes (2001) highlighted, those addicted to online sexual behaviour are at times adamant that their behaviour does not harm anyone and is all a 'virtual experience' (Carnes, 2001, p. 70). Our clinical experience supports this, as a frequent statement of abusers is that they were only masturbating to pictures, and Quayle and Taylor (2002) identify this in their research interviews: "It wasn't a person at all it was … it was just a flat image … it was a nothing" (p. 344). Consequently, behaviours ranging from passive membership of an online voyeurism fetish group, to viewing indecent images of children, may be easily maintained by an internet user, as they may not feel that they are committing the same wrongdoing for example, as someone physically spying on people undressing in their bedroom or abusing a child in person. Additionally, using the Triple-A-Engine (Cooper et al., 2004), accessibility encourages like-minded people to group together to engage in borderline or definitively illegal behaviour online, and this 'reduces the social stigma' (Wood, 2011, p. 136), and the anonymity of the internet hinders the attempts of law enforcement agents in identifying people perpetrating any deviance.

The above considers the issue of online-based offending, but if an individual offends offline, we might consider whether the mechanisms are the same. There are two important factors: whether the behaviour is successful, and whether the interaction fits with the expectations that have been developed through the consumption of pornography. Reiterating the importance of individual differences, pornography consumption can be comfortably maintained as a result of its capacity to meet a person's unique needs. Research recently identified that high levels of different personality traits in both men and women, as measured by the Big Five (Costa & McCrae, 1992) corresponded with problematic pornography use, but serving different functions: extraversion in men was positively associated with using pornography excessively to avoid negative feelings, but for women, this function of pornography use was most associated with narcissistic traits (Borgogna & Aita, 2019). For some, continuous offending may meet certain needs, so it is possible that an intention to offend that is unsuccessful or that does not meet a person's script could reduce the likelihood of further offending, but it might be viewed as 'training', which an individual can use to evolve their *modus operandi*. If it is successful, then the strategy is fulfilling a sexual need and is likely to be repeated; it may even be exacerbated if that behaviour fuels further fantasy and more nuanced pornographic consumption.

Escalation

As with other types of behaviour—including criminal behaviour—sexual crime can escalate in nature, frequency, and severity, and the likelihood of escalating a certain behaviour is influenced by several dispositional and situational factors. Following the influx of internet sexual material, questions have naturally been asked in recent years regarding pornography use and its possible catalytic effects on more serious, real-world behaviour. Wood (2011), writing from clinical experience and a psychodynamic perspective, detailed how escalation of sexual behaviour takes place through passing several 'thresholds'; initially using pornography casually, then compulsively, progressing onto illegal internet material, and eventually culminating in contact offending. This model can provide an explanation as to why viewers of mainstream, legal pornography can escalate their viewing preferences to pornography of an illegal nature, such as child pornography, despite reporting no paedophilic sexual attraction (Wood, 2011). However, we know that the number of users of online pornography is not the same as the number that use illegal pornography or go on to offend, which suggests that for escalation—as has previously been suggested for, for example, developing negative stereotypes of females—there are vulnerability factors (see Paul, 2009).

To further support or refute the claim that pornography has a role in the escalation of sexual offending, it is necessary to understand whether those who have committed offences report previous, prolonged pornography use, arguably alongside other sexual behaviours exhibiting a gradual increase in severity. A population of recent interest and importance in considering the role internet pornography has in the escalation of offending is those convicted of child-pornography offences (CPOs). The child-pornography industry is lucrative, and there are millions of images and videos circulating online. Given the magnitude of this content, it is useful to understand whether those who commit CPOs within the confines of the internet are likely to escalate their behaviour –to commit contact sexual offences against children—and whether those who have already perpetrated physical crimes against children represent those at the end of a criminal trajectory that began with viewing pornography. Seto et al. (2011) found that around 50% of their sample convicted of CPOs also reported contact sexual offences, and Bourke and Hernandez (2009) reached a similar conclusion, suggesting that internet offenders are significantly more likely to have committed a contact offense than to have not. While these studies, among others, reflect the crossover between these sexually deviant behaviours, the degree to which pornography causes such escalation is less well understood. Crucially, among Bourke and Hernandez's (2009) sample, the significant majority of dual offenders admitted to committing a contact offence against a child *before* engaging with child pornography, challenging the assumption that viewing child pornography automatically poses an escalatory risk.

Looking at recidivism figures and offence statistics, it was found by Seto and Eke (2005) that those who have previously used child pornography did not escalate to contact offences within a 2.5-year follow-up period, and further work has supported the separation of those who offend online and offline (Jung et al., 2012; Webb et al., 2007). As stated throughout this chapter, individual differences are important in determining arousal, pornography consumption, and offending behaviour, and they may be equally associated with escalation. Revisiting Williams et al.'s (2009) work, they stated that pornography is associated with a risk of activating sexually deviant behaviour for those *already* expressing certain personality traits; furthermore, the second study within their work demonstrated that a similar effect exists between pornography and *escalating* sexually deviant behaviour. Within the literature on those who escalate from using child pornography to contact abuse, a person's individual features are suggested to be the bridge across this gap. Interestingly, these factors are not exclusively related to arousal and sexual preference (i.e., paedophilic sexual preference, as one might expect), but those associated with wider criminality. For those experiencing paedophilia, the likelihood of escalating to contact crime was shown to be significantly higher when combined with a propensity for rule violation, antisocial traits, and diminished inhibitions towards offending (Babchishin et al., 2015), suggesting arousal towards children may not be independently sufficient to predict an escalation in deviant behaviour.

Beyond offending against children, Hewitt and Beauregard (2013) interviewed over 70 males convicted of a range of sexual offences against adults. They found that escalation of one's sexual criminality is dependent on several contextual variants: the victim's age, the degree to which the offence is premeditated, victim resistance, whether it is the first offence, and the location of the crime. Pornography or arousal were not cited as having an influence on their escalation within this sample; this does not mean that arousal is not implicated, but that the relationship between the internet, arousal, and an escalation in one's sexual deviance may be more multifaceted.

Conclusions

At present, any theoretical understanding of the role of the internet in arousal and sexual deviance has to be sensitive to the cohorts within which this type of research is conducted. Otherwise, we risk drawing conclusions from one non-digital generation and applying these to another generation, one whose technological exposure and access have been ever-present. Simply put, over 60% of young people now have constant internet access in their bedrooms, either on a handheld device or computer (Mascheroni & Olafsson, 2014—their data cover the age range

9–16 years from Denmark, Italy, Romania, Ireland, and the UK). This makes accessing pornography substantially easier than entering a shop at 18 years old, obtaining false identification, or asking someone older (such as a sibling) to purchase a magazine or video of a sexually explicit nature, as young people of previous generations were required to do. Additionally, these two opposing cohorts may have different attitudes towards pornography use based on society becoming more sexually tolerant and the increasing endorsement of sexually positive dialogue (Diamond, 2009). Couples who married twenty years ago, for example, may view pornography as something to be consumed when single and only when single; a survey report suggested that 75% of their female participants stated that they viewed pornography with their partner (Carroll et al., 2017). Today, however, individual masturbation and pornography use is encouraged by sexual-health professionals and celebrities such as the singer Lily Allen, who was recently announced as the face of a female sex-toy line, with the advertisement campaign focusing on solo female sexual pleasure, particularly within a relationship (Garvan, 2020); this is an attitude that may not have been promoted by previous generations.

The research that we have considered here suggests that pornography is a risk factor, but it is predominantly a risk factor for those individuals who are specifically vulnerable. The issue is that because the internet is so easily accessible, across generations and cultures, it is likely that more vulnerable people will be exposed to internet pornography, and this could thus result in an increase in offending behaviour. It is not possible to determine whether these vulnerable people would not offend or would still be vulnerable to offending if pornography was no longer available on the internet as it remains unclear if seeking pornography is a primary driver of vulnerability or is a consequence of it; nonetheless, this does not affect the debate on whether pornography is essentially inappropriate. What we are perhaps able to do is identify vulnerabilities in populations that do not have ready access to pornography via the internet or have had it curtailed for a period of time, determine their offending rate or proclivity to offend, and then examine how this might change as the internet is introduced.

References

Ahmed, F., Shafiq, M. Z., & Liu, A. X. (2016). The internet is for porn: Measurement and analysis of online adult traffic. *2016 IEEE 36th International Conference on Distributed Computing Systems (ICDCS)*, 88–97. https://doi.org/10.1109/ICDCS.2016.81

Allen, M., D'Alessio, D., & Brezgel, K. (1995). A meta-analysis summarizing the effects of pornography II: Aggression after exposure. *Human Communication Research, 22*, 258–283. https://doi.org/10.1111/j.1468-2958.1995.tb00368.x

Babchishin, K., Hanson, R. K., & VanZuylen, H. (2015). Online child pornography offenders are different: A meta-analysis of the characteristics of online and offline sex offenders against children. *Archives of Sexual Behaviour, 44*, 45–66.

Banjanin, N., Banjanin, N., Dimitrijevic, I., & Pantic, I. (2015). Relationship between internet use and depression: Focus on physiological mood oscillations, social networking and online addictive behavior. *Computers in Human Behavior, 43*, 308–312.

Barnett, G. D., & Mann, R. E. (2013a). Cognition, empathy, and sexual offending. *Trauma, Violence, & Abuse, 14*(1), 22–33.

Barnett, G., & Mann, R. E. (2013b). Empathy deficits and sexual offending: A model of obstacles to empathy. *Aggression and Violent Behaviour, 18*(2), 228–239.

Bauserman, R. (1996). Sexual aggression and pornography: A review of correlational research. *Basic and Applied Social Psychology, 8*, 405–427.

Bhuller, M., Havnes, T., Leuven, E., & Mogstad, M. (2013). Broadband internet: An information superhighway to sex crime? *Review of Economic Studies, 80*(4), 1237–1266.

Bonniwell, B. L. (1971). The social control of pornography and sexual behavior. *Annals of the American Academy of Political and Social Science, 397*(1), 97–104.

Borg, C., & de Jong, P. J. (2012). Feelings of disgust and disgust-induced avoidance weaken following induced sexual arousal in women. *PLoS ONE, 7*(9), Article e44111. https://doi.org/10.1371/journal.pone.0044111

Borgogna, N. C., & Aita, S. L. (2019). Problematic pornography viewing from a Big-5 personality, perspective: Sexual addiction & compulsivity. *The Journal of Treatment & Prevention, 26*(3–4), 293–314.

Bourke, M. L., & Hernandez, A. E. (2009). The 'Butner Study' redux: A report of the incidence of hands-on child victimization by child pornography offenders. *Journal of Family Violence, 24*(3), 183–191.

Brand, M., Laier, C., Pawlikowski, M., Schächtle, U., Schöler, T., & Altstötter-Gleich, C. (2011). Watching pornographic pictures on the internet: Role of sexual arousal ratings and psychological-psychiatric symptoms for using

internet sex sites excessively. *Cyberpsychology, Behavior, and Social Networking, 14*, 371–377. https://doi.org/10.1089/cyber.2010.0222
Brosius, H. B., Weaver, J. B., & Staab, J. F. (1993). Exploring the social and sexual 'reality' of contemporary pornography. *Journal of Sex Research, 30*(2), 161–170.
Bryant, P. (2009). Predicting internet pornography use and arousal: The role of individual difference variables. *The Journal of Sex Research, 46*(4), 344–357. https://doi.org/10.1016/0191-8869(92)90236-I
Carnes, P. (2001). *Out of the shadows: Understanding sexual addiction*. Hazelden Publishing.
Carroll, J. S., Busby, D. M., Willoughby, B. J., & Brown, C. C. (2017). The porn gap: Differences in men's and women's pornography patterns in couple relationships. *Journal of Couple & Relationship Therapy, 16*(2), 146–163.
Cooper, A., McLoughlin, I. P., & Campbell, K. M. (2004). Sexuality in cyberspace: Update for the 21st century. *CyberPsychology & Behavior, 3*(4), 521–536.
Costa, P. T., & McCrae, R. R. (1992). Four ways five factors are basic. *Personality and Individual Differences, 13*, 653–665.
Cronin, B. (2008). Eros unbound: Pornography and the internet. In W. Asprey & P. Ceruzzi (Eds.), *The internet and American business: An historic investigation* (pp. 491–528). MIT Press.
De Almeida Neto, A. C., Eyland, S., Ware, J., Galouzis, J., & Kevin, M. (2011). Internet sexual offending: Overview of potential contributing factors and intervention strategies. *Psychiatry, Psychology and Law, 20*(2), 168–181.
Demaré, D., Briere, J., & Lips, H. M. (1988). Violent pornography and self-reported likelihood of sexual aggression. *Journal of Research in Personality, 22*(2), 140–153.
Diamond, M. (2009). Pornography, public acceptance and sex related crime: A review. *International Journal of Law and Psychiatry, 32*, 304–314.
Diamond, M., Jozifkova, E., & Wiess, P. (2011). Pornography and sex crimes in the Czech republic. *Archives of Sexual Behaviour, 40*, 1037–1043.
Diegmann, A. (2019). The internet effects on sex crime offenses: Evidence from the German broadband internet expansion. *Journal of Economic Behavior and Organization, 165*, 82–99.
Donnerstein, E., Linz, D., & Penrod, S. (1987). *The question of pornography: Research findings and policy implications*. Free Press.
Easterbrook, J. A. (1959). The effect of emotion on cue utilization and the organization of behavior. *Psychological Review, 66*(3), 183–201. https://doi.org/10.1037/h0047707
Efrati, Y., Shukron, O., & Epstein, R. (2019). Compulsive sexual behaviour and sexual offending: Differences in cognitive schemas, sensation seeking, and impulsivity. *Journal of Behavioural Addictions, 8*(3), 432–441.

Finn, S. (1997). Origins of media exposure: Linking personality traits to TV, radio, print, and film use. *Communication Research, 24*, 507–529.

Foley, J. P. (2020). Ethics in internet. *Journal of Interdisciplinary Studies, 32*(1/2), 179–192.

Garvan, S. (2020, October 31). 'I'm the friend who recommends you sex toys'. *BBC News*. https://www.bbc.co.uk/news/newsbeat-54712504

Gehl, R. W. (2016). Power/freedom on the dark web: A digital ethnography of the dark web social network. *New Media & Society, 18*(7), 1219–1235.

Hald, G. M., & Malamuth, N. M. (2015). Experimental effects of exposure to pornography: The moderating effect of personality and mediating effect of sexual arousal. *Archives of Sexual Behaviour, 44*, 99–109.

Hald, G. M., Malamuth, N. M., & Lange, T. (2013). Pornography and sexist attitudes among heterosexuals. *Journal of Communication, 63*(4), 638–660.

Hald, G. M., Seaman, C., & Linz, D. (2014). Sexuality and pornography. In D. Tolman, L. Diamond, J. Bauermeister, W. George, J. Pfaus, & M. Ward (Eds.), *APA Handbook of sexuality and psychology* (pp. 3–35). American Psychological Association.

Hare, R. D. (1982). Psychopathy and the personality dimensions of psychoticism, extraversion and neuroticism. *Personality and Individual Differences, 3*, 35–42.

Hewitt, A., & Beauregard, E. (2013). Offending patterns of serial sex offenders: Escalation, de-escalation and consistency of sexually intrusive and violent behaviours. *Journal of Investigative Psychology and Offender Profiling, 11*, 57–80. https://doi.org/10.1002/jip.1407

Hogarth, L. (2020). Addiction is driven by excessive goal-directed drug choice under negative affect: Translational critique of habit and compulsion theory. *Neuropsychopharmacology, 45*(5), 720–735.

Hollis, V., Belton, E., & Team, N. E. (2017). *Children and young people who engage in technology-assisted harmful sexual behaviour*. National Society for the Prevention of Cruelty to Children.

Hughes, A., Brewer, G., & Khan, R. (2020). Sexual coercion by women: The influence of pornography and narcissistic and histrionic personality disorder traits. *Archives of Sexual Behaviour, 49*, 885–894.

Jensen-Campbell, L. A., & Graziano, W. G. (2001). Agreeableness as a moderator of interpersonal conflict. *Journal of Personality, 69*(2), 323–362.

Joyce, R. A. (2008). Pornography and the internet. *IEEE Internet Computing, 12*(4), 74–77. https://doi.org/10.1109/MIC.2008.83

Jung, S., Ennis, L., Stein, S., Choy, A. L., & Hook, T. (2012). Child pornography possessors: Comparisons and contrasts with contact- and non-contact sex offenders. *Journal of Sexual Aggression, 19*(3), 295–310. https://doi.org/10.1080/13552600.2012.741267

Kendall, T. (2006). *Pornography, rape, and the internet*. https://idei.fr/sites/default/files/medias/doc/conf/sic/papers_2007/kendall.pdf
Kimmel, M. S., & Linders, A. (1996). Does censorship make a difference: An aggregate empirical analysis of pornography and rape. *Journal of Psychology and Human Sexuality, 8*(3), 1–20.
Kunaharan, S., Halpin, S., Sitharthan, T., Bosshard, S., & Walla, P. (2017). Conscious and non-conscious measures of emotion: Do they vary with frequency of pornography use? *Applied Science, 7*(5), 493–509.
Laier, C., Pawlikowski, M., & Brand, M. (2014). Sexual picture processing interferes with decision-making under ambiguity. *Archives of Sexual Behavior, 43*, 473–482. https://doi.org/10.1007/s10508-013-0119-8
Laier, C., Pawlikowski, M., Pekal, J., Schulte, F. P., & Brand, M. (2013). Cybersex addiction: Experienced sexual arousal when watching pornography and not real-life sexual contacts makes the difference. *Journal of Behavioral Addictions, 2*(2), 100–107. https://doi.org/10.1556/jba.2.2013.002
Landripet, I., Buško, V., & Štulhofer, A. (2019). Testing the content progression thesis: A longitudinal assessment of pornography use and preference for coercive and violent content among male adolescents. *Social Science Research, 81*, 32–41. https://doi.org/10.1016/j.ssresearch.2019.03.003
Lo, V.-H., & Wei, R. (2005). Exposure to internet pornography and Taiwanese adolescents' sexual attitudes and behavior. *Journal of Broadcasting & Electronic Media, 49*(2), 221–237. https://doi.org/10.1207/s15506878jobem4902_5
Marshall, W. L., Seidman, B. T., & Barbaree, H. E. (1988). The effects of prior exposure to erotic and nonerotic stimuli on the rape index. *Sexual Abuse: A Journal of Research and Treatment, 4*, 209–220.
Mascheroni, G., & Olafsson, K. (2014). *Net children go mobile: Risks and opportunities*. Second edition. Educatt. http://www.netchildrengomobile.eu/wp-content/uploads/2013/07/Ncgm_Full.pdf
Miller, D., & Slater, D. (2020). *The Internet: An ethnographic approach*. Routledge.
Moretta, T., & Buodo, G. (2020). Problematic internet use and loneliness: How complex is the relationship? A short literature review. *Current Addiction Reports, 7*(2), 125–136.
Mosher, D. J. (1988). Pornography defined: Sexual involvement theory, narrative context, and goodness-of-fit. *Journal of Psychology & Human Sexuality, 1*(1), 67–85.
Nolte, A. (2017). The internet effects on sex crime and murder: Evidence from the broadband internet expansion in Germany. *Social Science Research Network*. http://ftp.zew.de/pub/zew-docs/dp/dp17050.pdf
Ogas, O., & Gaddam, S. (2012). *A billion wicked thoughts: What the internet tells us about sex and relationships*. Plume.

Paul, B. (2009). Predicting internet pornography use and arousal: The role of individual difference variables. *Journal of Sex Research, 46*(4), 344–357.

Peter, J., & Valkenburg, P. M. (2008). Adolescents' exposure to sexually explicit internet material and sexual preoccupancy: A three-way panel study. *Media Psychology, 11*, 207–234.

Pew Internet Project. (2000, May 10). *Tracking online life: How women use the internet to cultivate relationships with family and friends*. https://www.pewresearch.org/internet/2000/05/10/tracking-online-life-how-women-use-the-internet-to-cultivate-relationships-with-family-and-friends/

Ponzanesi, S. (2020). Digital diasporas: Postcoloniality, media and affect. *Interventions, 22*(8), 977–993. https://doi.org/10.1080/1369801X.2020.1718537

Price, J., Patterson, R., Regnerus, M., & Walley, J. (2016). How much more XXX is generation X consuming? Evidence of changing attitudes and behaviors related to pornography since 1973. *Journal of Sex Research, 53*(1), 12–20. https://doi.org/10.1080/00224499.2014.1003773

Quayle, E., & Taylor, M. (2002). Child pornography and the internet: Perpetuating a cycle of abuse. *Deviant Behavior, 23*(4), 331–361.

Rea, M. C. (2001). What is pornography? *Noûs, 35*(1), 118–145.

Righthand, S., & Welch, C. (2013). Characteristics of youth who sexually offend. In K. Crumpton Franey (Eds.), *Identifying and treating youth who sexually offend: Current approaches, techniques, and research*, 15–32.

Rimer, J. R. (2016). Internet sexual offending from an anthropological perspective: Analysing offender perceptions of online spaces. *Journal of Sexual Aggression, 23*(1), 33–45.

Rostad, W. L., Gittins-Stone, D., Huntington, C., Rizzo, C. J., Pearlman, D., & Orchowski, L. (2019). The association between exposure to violent pornography and teen dating violence in grade 10 high school students. *Archives of Sexual Behavior, 48*(7), 2137–2147. https://doi.org/10.1007/s10508-019-1435-4

Rothman, E. F., Kaczmarsky, C., Burke, N., Jansen, E., & Baughman, A. (2015). 'Without porn… I wouldn't know half the things I know now': A qualitative study of pornography use among a sample of urban, low-income, black and Hispanic youth. *The Journal of Sex Research, 52*(7), 736–746.

Rubin, A. M. (1994). Media uses and effects: A uses and gratifications perspectives. In J. Bryant & D. Zillman (Eds.), *Media effects: Advances in theory and research* (pp. 417–436). Lawrence Erlbaum Associates Inc.

Rupp, H. A., & Wallen, K. (2008). Sex differences in response to visual sexual stimuli: A review. *Archives of Sexual Behavior, 37*, 206–218. https://doi.org/10.1007/s10508-007-9217-9

Seigfried-Spellar, K. C., & Rogers, M. K. (2013). Does deviant pornography use follow a guttman-like progression? *Computers in Human Behavior, 29*, 1997–2003. https://doi.org/10.1016/j.chb.2013.04.018

Seto, M. C., & Eke, A. W. (2005). The criminal histories and later offending of child pornography offenders. *Sexual Abuse: A Journal of Research and Treatment, 17*, 201–210.

Seto, M. C., Hanson, R. K., & Babchishin, K. M. (2011). Contact sexual offending by men with online sexual offences. *Sexual Abuse: A Journal of Research and Treatment, 23*, 124–145.

Seto, M. C., Maric, A., & Barbaree, H. E. (2001). The role of pornography in the etiology of sexual aggression. *Aggression and Violent Behaviour, 6*(1), 35–53.

Shor, E., & Seida, K. (2019). "Harder and harder"? Is mainstream pornography becoming increasingly violent and do viewers prefer violent content? *The Journal of Sex Research, 56*(1), 16–28.

Stalans, L. J., & Finn, M. A. (2016). Understanding how the internet facilitates crime and deviance. *Victims and Offenders: An International Journal of Evidence-Based Research, Policy and Practice, 11*(4), 501–508.

Stanley, N., Barter, C., Wood, M., Aghtaie, N., Larkins, C., Lanau, A., & Överlien, C. (2018). Pornography, sexual coercion and abuse and sexting in young people's intimate relationships: A European study. *Journal of Interpersonal Violence, 33*(19), 2919–2944.

Suler, J. (2004). The online disinhibition effect. *CyberPsychology & Behavior, 7*(3), 321–326.

Tanner-Smith, E. E., Wilson, S. J., & Lipsey, M. W. (2013). Risk factors and crime. In F. T. Cullen & P. Wilcox (Eds.), *The oxford handbook of criminological theory* (pp. 89–115). Oxford University Press.

Tsaliki, L. (2015). Popular culture and moral panics about 'children at risk': Revisiting the sexualisation-of-young-girls debate. *Sex Education, 15*(5), 500–514. https://doi.org/10.1080/14681811.2015.1022893

Van den Bergh, B., Dewitte, S., & Warlop, L. (2008). Bikinis instigate generalized impatience in intertemporal choice. *Journal of Consumer Research, 35*(1), 85–97.

Vega, V., & Malamuth, N. M. (2007). Predicting sexual aggression: The role of pornography in the context of general and specific risk factors. *Aggressive Behaviour, 33*, 104–117.

Ward, T., & Beech, A. R. (2016). The integrated theory of sexual offending–revised: A multifield perspective. *The Wiley handbook on the theories, assessment and treatment of sexual offending*, 123–137.

Webb, L., Craissati, J., & Keen, S. (2007). Characteristics of internet child pornography offenders: A comparison with child molesters. *Sexual Abuse: A*

Journal of Research and Treatment, 19, 449–465. https://doi.org/10.1177/1079063207019004 08

Williams, K. M. (2002). *Discriminating the dark triad of personality (T)*. University of British Columbia. Retrieved from https://open.library.ubc.ca/collections/ubctheses/831/items/1.0090536

Williams, K. M., Cooper, B. S., Howell, T. M., Yuille, J. C., & Paulhus, D. L. (2009). Inferring sexually deviant behavior from corresponding fantasies: The role of personality and pornography consumption. *Criminal Justice and Behavior, 36*(2), 198–222.

Winick, C., & Evans, J. T. (1996). The relationship between nonenforcement of state pornography laws and rates of sex crime arrests. *Archives of Sexual Behavior, 25*(5), 439–453.

Wood, H. (2011). The internet and its role in the escalation of sexually compulsive behaviour. *Psychoanalytic Psychotherapy, 25*(2), 127–142.

Wouda, J. C., Hartman, P. M., Bakker, R. M., Bakker, J. O., van de Wiel, H. B. M., & Weijmar Schultz, W. C. M. (1998). Vaginal plethysmography in women with dyspareunia. *Journal of Sex Research, 35*(2), 141–147. https://doi.org/10.1080/00224499809551927

Wright, P. J. (2013). U.S. males and pornography, 1973–2010: Consumption, predictors, correlates. *Journal of Sex Research, 50*(1), 60–71.

Wulfert, E., Roland, B. D., Hartley, J., Wang, J., & Franco, C. (2005). Heart rate arousal and excitement in gambling: Winners versus losers. *Psychology of Addictive Behaviors, 19*(3), 311–316. https://doi.org/10.1037/0893-164X.19.3.311

Ybarra, M. L., & Mitchell, K. J. (2005). Exposure to Internet pornography among children and adolescents: A national survey. *Cyberpsychology & Behavior, 8*(5), 473–486.

Ybarra, M. L., Strasburger, V. C., & Mitchell, K. J. (2014). Sexual media exposure, sexual behaviour and sexual violence victimization in adolescence. *Clinical Pediatrics, 53*, 1239–1247.

Yerkes, R. M., & Dodson, J. D. (1908). The relation of strength of stimulus to rapidity of habit-formation. *Journal of Comparative Neurology and Psychology, 18*(5), 459–482. https://doi.org/10.1002/cne.920180503

Young, K. S. (2008). Internet sex addiction: Risk factors, stages of development, and treatment. *American Behavioral Scientist, 52*, 21–37. https://doi.org/10.1177/0002764208321339

CHAPTER 2

Child Sexual Exploitation Material: Motivations for Use and Implications for Deterrence, Treatment, and Prevention

Derek Perkins, Sarah Wefers, and Rosa Dreyhaupt

Introduction

Child sexual exploitation material (CSEM) is an overarching category that includes still or moving photographic or non-photographic images depicting child sexual abuse, and written material, such as so-called 'pedophile manuals' and pornographic narratives about child sexual

D. Perkins (✉)
Royal Holloway University of London, Egham, England
e-mail: derek.perkins@rhul.ac.uk

S. Wefers
Lucy Faithfull Foundation, Bromsgrove, England
e-mail: S.Wefers@shu.ac.uk

R. Dreyhaupt
Deutsche Gesellschaft Für Verhaltenstherapie, Tübingen, Germany
e-mail: rosa.dreyhaupt@posteo.de

C. A. Harper et al. (eds.), *Sexual Crime and the Internet*, Sexual Crime,
https://doi.org/10.1007/978-3-031-95844-1_2

abuse. Indecent images of children (IIOC) is the largest sub-category of CSEM.

Another sub-category of visual CSEM is 'non-photographic sexual abuse imagery' (NPAI) depicting children or childlike characters. This is legally referred to as Prohibited Images of Children and includes computer-generated images, cartoons and drawings focused solely or principally on a child's genitals or anal region, or portrays one or more listed sexual acts involving, or carried out in the presence of a child. Possession is subject to legal sanctions under the Coroners and Justice Act 2009 (England and Wales) if these images are deemed to be 'pornographic (meaning produced for the purpose of sexual arousal), grossly offensive, disgusting or otherwise obscene'.

The possession, distribution, or production of IIOC is increasing rapidly, outstripping the capacity of traditional law enforcement approaches to tackle the problem within detection, arrest, conviction, and sentencing. The term child pornography has appropriately been gradually replaced by IIOC and CSEM to reflect the true nature of the material, namely child sexual abuse imagery. However, the term child pornography is still retained in some international legal terminology and therefore occasionally appears in this chapter in that context.

In many Western countries, such as the United States, Canada, and several European countries, IIOC offending attracts severe penalties. In the US, for example, federal laws impose mandatory minimum sentences ranging from 5 to 20 years for possession, distribution, or production of child pornography, with enhancements for repeat offenders. Canada also has stringent laws, with penalties of up to 14 years for possession and distribution, and up to 14 years for making child pornography. In England and Wales, sentences range from a community order through to 9 years imprisonment, depending on the circumstances and type of images involved. Indecent images of a child (i.e., depicting someone under 18) are defined as images of naked or partially clothed children or children posing sexually, which can include self-generated imagery, for example, through 'sexting' by minors (Internet Watch Foundation, 2022). The most extreme images (Category A) include penetrative and violent sexual activity against children, for which there is a maximum of 3 years' imprisonment for 'possession' and a minimum 6 years imprisonment for 'making'. Lesser sentences apply for Category B images, comprising non-penetrative sexual activity and Category C images, comprising children on their own, for which a community order may be applied. Similar sanctions of imprisonment also apply in the Germany, France, USA, Canada, New Zealand, and Australia.

In comparison, some other jurisdictions have not yet established comprehensive laws for CSEM offending, including some regions in the Middle East and some Pacific Island nations, resulting in an absence of formal penalties. This is particularly so for countries with limited resources for law enforcement or where cultural taboos prevent open discussions about sexual abuse. International treaties, such as The Council of Europe Convention on Protection of Children against Sexual Exploitation and Sexual Abuse, known as 'the Lanzarote Convention' (Council of Europe, 2007), and the Optional Protocol on the Sale of Children, Child Prostitution and Child Pornography (United Nations, 2000), have aimed to harmonise legal standards across countries and promote stricter punishments. However, implementation varies, and compliance can be inconsistent.

The volume of CSEM online is increasing. In 2023, the Internet Watch Foundation (IWF, 2024) assessed 392,665 reports of child sexual abuse images or videos, which was an increase of 5% compared to 2022. These mostly involve girls but images of boys are disproportionally more violent. Of the 275,652 webpages actioned by the IWF during 2023, 92% were assessed as containing 'self-generated' imagery, mostly involving children aged 11–13, which is a 14% increase in 2022. As noted by the IWF, the term self-generated imagery is potentially misleading as it includes children being groomed, deceived, or extorted into producing and sharing sexual images or videos.

Creating and accessing IIOC is increasingly carried out on mobile devices, such as smartphones or tablets, and on many platforms (Protect Children, 2024; Roser et al., 2015). Adults seeking this material, for their own gratification and/or to swap with other users, feeds the cycle of abuse. Access to such internet-connected mobile devices by increasingly younger children also places them at risk of accessing IIOC, deliberately or accidentally and/or being sexually exploited online. In a sample of dark web and CSEM users, 40% reported that they first came across CSEM when they were 13 years old or younger (Protect Children, 2024). Of a cohort of boys assessed by the NSPCC who had displayed harmful sexual behaviour, almost a half had been involved in some form of 'technology assisted' online sexually harmful behaviour (Hackett et al., 2019), indicating an association between online image-based behaviour and other harmful behaviours.

Types of CSEM

As mentioned above, several subtypes of CSEM exist. Merdian et al. (2022) carried out a systematic review and Delphi expert survey of NPAI. They concluded that a) there is no universally agreed definition of NPAI and called for an international consensus on defining and tackling NPAI; and b) potential harms of NPAI include being used to groom children, reinforcing distorted attitudes about child sexual abuse, and desensitising viewers to such abuse, although it is noted that there is limited research evidence on this. They advocated restricting children's access to online pornography and improving their education about healthy relationships.

The use of artificial intelligence further posits risks for the creating of CSEM. The recent Threat Assessment by the National Crime Agency (2023) identified the use of virtual and augmented reality as an emerging threat. The Internet Watch Foundation (2023) investigated over 11,000 AI images distributed on a dark web child sexual abuse forum within just one month. They noted that AI images are becoming difficult to distinguish from real recordings and that images of real children had been morphed into child abuse material. This indicated the risk posed to real children by the use of AI. Online CSEM offending, due to access anonymity, the rise of online forums, and desensitisation to existing material, feeds the demand for more and new CSEM material and has morphed in some instances into live streaming of child sexual abuse (Skidmore et al., 2022; Ramiro et al, 2019).

Live Streaming of Child Sexual Abuse

There is an increasing global threat posed by live streaming of child sexual abuse (Brown et al., 2020; Varella, 2017). Instead of solely using static CSEM, easily available technology now enables offenders to view and exploit children live via webcam (de Tribolet-Hardy et al., 2020). This often involves offenders directing the explicit behaviour that children engage in or they may also direct a facilitator to abuse children in front of the webcam. Offenders can hence shape the abuse, directly communicate with victims and facilitators and request specific live images that reflect their individual interests (Açar, 2017).

Although live streaming offences may occur in any country, children in poorer countries are particularly vulnerable to being exploited for live streaming offences (WePROTECT Global Alliance, 2019). Offenders in richer countries can easily initiate contact with vulnerable children or facilitators in other countries (ECPAT, 2017). Live streaming of child sexual abuse is therefore often a transnational offence with the offender residing in a different country compared to the child victim. The Philippines has been identified as a major source of live-streamed child sexual abuse (EUROPOL, 2016; National Crime Agency, 2019), influenced by factors including poverty, high internet connectivity, the wide availability of cheap electronic devices that can be used for video chats, English proficiency and cultural expectations in Southeast Asia that children should contribute to family income (Varella, 2017; Christensen & Woods, 2024). Due to the established commercial sex industry, online commercial sexual exploitation may be considered an easy and feasible way of making money (Ramiro et al., 2019), which could be seen as less abusive than commercial sexual exploitation on the streets. Facilitators, who are often family members of the child victims, have also reported that they consider live-streamed offences less abusive because there is no physical contact between the offenders and the children (WePROTECT Global Alliance, 2019).

In a study of factors involved in the Online Sexual Abuse and Exploitation of Children (OSAEC) in the Philippines, Munns et al. (2024) provided an analysis of interviews with convicted and incarcerated OSAEC facilitation offenders. This highlighted the role of financial transactions linked to OSAEC and chat log interactions between foreign perpetrators and local facilitators of OSAEC, which enhanced understanding of the varied individual, family, community, social and technological issues that motivated offenders to facilitate OSAEC in the Philippines. As outlined above, the primary motive was extreme poverty, which drove individuals to engage in OSAEC as a means of financially supporting their families. The community environment also normalised this activity, with many seeing it as an 'easy' way to earn money, and participants often rationalised their involvement by believing they were not causing direct physical harm since interactions were virtual. Additionally, the transactional relationship with foreign perpetrators, who primarily sought interactions with minors, further facilitated and perpetuated this abuse. Better understanding of how these offences were carried out identified ways in which they can be better detected, deterred and prevented.

Even though live streaming offences are hands-off online child sexual exploitation offences, the type and format of the interaction indicates a quality that is more akin to hands-on child sexual offences compared to other online child sexual exploitation offences, such as the viewing of CSEM (de Tribolet-Hardy et al., 2020). However, research on live streaming offenders is largely lacking (Brown et al., 2020) and therefore, such offending may require a less structured risk assessment exploring their individual risk factors, as no structured risk assessment tool has been developed (de Tribolet-Hardy et al., 2020). Emerging evidence suggests that people who livestream abuse are mostly men from rich Western countries, who are approximately 40 years old (Kleijn & Bogaerts, 2019; Kuhlmann & Auren, 2015). Investigations of Australian live streaming offenders suggested that repeated offenders tend to escalate in their offending (Brown et al., 2020). This was indicated by shorter durations between offences and increased amounts of money sent abroad over their course of live streaming offences. EUROPOL (2016) further noted a large overlap between live streaming offences and travelling abroad to abuse children; and Cubitt et al. (2023) identified a subgroup of live streaming offenders who also engaged in contact abuse. This raises the question of whether live streaming offenders have a different psychological and risk profile compared to exclusive CSEM offenders.

A final important note is the current lack of explicit criminalisation of live streaming of child sexual abuse within international legal frameworks. ECPAT International is a global organisation specifically dedicated to ending child sexual exploitation and they are involved in campaigning for clear legalisation against child sexual abuse. They are a useful resource for understanding how different countries define child sexual abuse in legal contexts and whether or not this is in line with international standards (ECPAT, n.d.).

Pathways to and Motivations for CSEM Offending

Trajectories into CSEM offending have been investigated over recent years. Motives for the creation of IIOC, as well as use for sexual gratification, include financial gain, trading with other CSEM users and as a means to be accepted into networks of users of CSEM (Liggett et al., 2020). Studies of those who have accessed CSEM have identified the role of early life experiences in their pathways to offending, often multi-faceted offence motivations and a range of situational factors triggering various cognitive and emotional responses. Merdian et al., (2013a, 2013b) set out a range of reasons for their offending given by those convicted of CSEM offending, highlighting the wide range of functions that the behaviour served for them. These reasons may not, of course, be mutually exclusive and may change over time (Fig. 2.1).

Merdian et al., (2013a, 2013b) also distinguished between fantasy-driven and contact-driven CSEM offending. Whilst fantasy-driven use of CSEM served solely to facilitate sexual fantasies, contact-driven use of CSEM related to facilitating contact with children so as to carry out contact sexual abuse. Those engaging in both types of offending—accessing CSEM and contact sexual offending—were found to be the most generally antisocial in meta-analyses of studies involving CSEM-only, contact-only and mixed (CSEM plus contact) offending (Babchishin et al. 2011, 2015).

Middleton et al. (2006) tested the applicability of the Ward and Siegert (2002) Pathways Model of Sexual Offending to a sample of men convicted of IIOC offences. Of the 72 cases drawn from a community sample in England and Wales, 60% displayed 'dysfunctional psychological

Serves as a collectible	Has commercial value
Functions as online currency	Facilitates social relationships
A means of escaping from the real world	An expression of a risk taking lifestyle
An expression of general criminal lifestyle	Serves sexual gratification
Serves sexual exploration/experimentation	Serves as therapy
Interactive tool in victim grooming	Serves as template for real-life sexual abuse
A means of blackmailing a victim	To keep as a trophy of abuse

Fig. 2.1 Self-reported reasons for accessing CSEM (Merdian et al., 2013a, 2013b)

mechanisms', notably the 'intimacy deficits pathway', and the 'emotional dysregulation pathway'. Merdian et al. (2018) similarly described different pathways to CSEM offending—based on detailed interviews, psychometric assessment and use of implicit measures of sexual interest—with 20 men who acknowledged their CSEM offending and were in psychological interventions. They summarised participants' main offence-related personal vulnerabilities, which were linked to early life experiences, as *Socioemotional dysfunctionality*"—i.e., negative internal states, dysfunctional coping and sexual interest in children—consistent with the emotional and intimacy difficulties identified by Middleton et al. (2006). These personal vulnerabilities were described as interacting with *Personal Circumstances*, *Permission-Giving Thoughts*, and the *Internet Environment* in generating offending behaviour.

Based on a review of previous studies, Bartels and Merdian (2016) conceptualised the first set of implicit theories that may be unique to CSEM offenders, namely: *Unhappy World* (the world as a negative and rejecting place), *Self as Uncontrollable* (external factors that are out of one's control affect one's behaviour), *Nature of Harm (CSEM variant)* (CSEM offending as less harmful than hands-on abuse), *Children as Sex Objects* (children are objects that can be used for one's sexual gratification), and *Self as Collector* (CSEM collection as a booster for one's social status).

Merdian et al. (2020) combined existing theory and empirical knowledge of CSEM offending, with their own research with CSEM offenders in treatment (Merdian et al., 2018) to develop an assessment tool—the CSEM Pathways Tool (CPT)—aimed at increasing understanding of an individual's pathway to their offending behaviour that is both (a) comprehensive (establishing links between past, present, and likely future behaviour, and between personal attributes and situational factors) and (b) collaborative, in that the exploration and analysis of the offence pathway is a shared process between the client and the clinician. Findings indicated that the CPT was considered a useful addition to treatment by both treatment participants and facilitators. Participants reported increased understanding of their offending behaviour that was useful in supporting desistance but recommended greater individualisation of the CPT to their unique circumstances.

In a qualitative study (Dreyhaupt, 2020), 40 self-identified CSEM offenders reported on their individual and situational circumstances surrounding the initiation and continuation of their offences. Most commonly, participants reported that their *Sexual Interest in Children or Adolescents* made them seek out CSEM in the first place, whilst others described CSEM as an outlet for other sexual fantasies. In the latter group, the sexual motivation to access CSEM was more general, in the sense that it allowed the men to engage with their individual sexual orientation, fantasies, or past sexual experiences. For example, they cited reminiscences of their own sexual experiences as a child as a driver to engage in offending behaviour. Another male participant articulated that accessing CSEM was his way of coping with his presumably homosexual orientation and sexual desires.

Participants commonly perceived the onset of their CSEM offending behaviour to be a direct result of their *Coping Strategies with Adverse Living Conditions* such as stress, depressed mood, loneliness, or job and relationship problems at the time. The theme of *Desensitisation* was mentioned by about a third of the participants: they reportedly started with the use of legal pornography depicting adults and eventually proceeded to access CSEM. A prominent notion was that legal pornography at one point did not suffice anymore to fulfil its individual rewarding function, so the participants perceived an increased need for stimulation and transgressed to CSEM. Problematic use of legal adult pornography has been identified as an important contributor to CSEM use by other authors (Bailey et al., 2022).

Both the onset and maintenance of viewing CSEM appeared to have been facilitated by a sense of *Alienation from Agency*, where participants attributed their behaviour to allegedly uncontrollable internal characteristics and/or external circumstances (especially the Internet environment), thereby reducing the element of conscious control and intent of their actions (Dreyhaupt, 2020). Similarly, the theme *Minimisation of Harm and Wrongfulness* was displayed by some participants who reported attitudes that pointed towards a justification of their behaviour by claiming their actions to be harmless due to the perceived passiveness of merely viewing the material and not actively engaging in its production or distribution. Lastly, it appeared that CSEM offending behaviour was maintained through some kind of *Reinforcement*: on the one hand, the Internet environment itself seemed to possess certain features that reinforced the offending behaviour of some individuals by providing easy access and sufficient anonymity as well as a means to escape from everyday life. On the other hand, the associated sexual and non-sexual arousal drove future offending behaviour.

Functions of CSEM use may change over time and there can be different factors involved in the onset and the maintenance of CSEM offending behaviour. Those factors are not always clearly separable and may interact and, thus, increase chances to engage in CSEM offending behaviour (Fig. 2.2).

Effects of the COVID-19 Pandemic

The advent and the course of the COVID-19 pandemic led to changes not only in the global economy but also in the social and working lives of many people around the world. Public health measures such as school closures and curfews led to an increase in time spent at home and thus, time spent online (Kemp et al., 2021). Concerns were expressed about children being increasingly exposed to offenders online via chats or online games due to unsupervised internet access, heightening the risk for online grooming and sexual exploitation (ECPAT, 2020; EUROPOL, 2021; UNICEF, 2020). Moreover, due to the travel restrictions related to the pandemic, (potential) travelling sex offenders are believed to have engaged in increased online child sexual exploitation for their sexual gratification (INTERPOL, 2020). Indeed, available country-level data suggest that there has been an increase in blocked attempts to access CSEM-related websites in EU member states during the respective lockdowns as well as increased CSEM-sharing in peer-to-peer networks (Europol, 2020; Internet Watch Foundation, 2022).

Not only did the regulations of the COVID-19 pandemic increase the risk for children to be sexually exploited online but it also had an impact on CSEM offenders. Between April and September 2020, the largest child sexual abuse prevention helpline worldwide, 'Stop It Now UK &Ireland', recorded that around 10% of the callers were explicitly concerned about the impact of COVID-19 on their own sexual thoughts or behaviour towards children (Naldrett et al., 2021). A recent qualitative study explored the effects of the COVID-19 pandemic on individuals who access child sexual abuse material (McMahan et al., 2023). Participants were recruited from the internet-based CBT intervention 'Prevent It' which is designed for individuals who currently access CSEM and would like to stop. Results suggest that besides changes to day-to-day life associated with the pandemic (e.g., working from home, decreased social activities), participants disclosed changes in sexual thoughts, feelings and behaviours that included increasing urges and actions to access CSEM

This is a composite case; it does not describe any personally identifiable individual but contains elements from various individuals the authors have seen.

David, aged 32, grew up in a family home in which there were regular conflicts between his parents. As a young child, he heard them arguing and shouting and he witnessed some physical violence from his father towards his mother, pushing and shoving her. He felt anxious about what was happening, wished that he could do something about it and ultimately felt guilty about not being able to make things better. David learned to cope with this by turning off his feelings.

From age 13, he was able to distract himself from these family problems by spending time with his best friend next door and with his 5 years' older brother, with whom he had very good relationships. When his older brother was 18, he joined the Army, which coincided with David's best friend moving away with his family to another town, leaving David feeling bereft.

David was bullied at school and witnessed sexual harassment of girls in and outside school. He later recalled being excited by seeing girls in this situation but also being ashamed of his feelings. He began truanting from school and spent time at home alone, where he discovered his father's collection of pornography, to which he began masturbating, often imagining the pubescent girls from his school. This was both arousing and distracting from his emotional problems. He later recalled his father, realising that David had found this material, giving him "a nod and a wink" to indicate that this was ok.

Eventually David's distress about being bullied came to the notice of his mother, who said she would speak to the school but this turned out not to have happened, all of which left David feeling that he could not trust people with sensitive information. David continued throughout his teenage years viewing online pornography, partly as a way of escaping his emotional problems and found himself drawn to material involving pubescent girls, of about the same age of the girls he had witnessed being sexually harassed at school.

After two unsuccessful short-term relationships, David settled into a relationship with Emma, of the same age and they were married at the age of 23. Although David had reduced his pornography use, he regularly relapsed into secretly using it at night at times of work, social or marital problems. When arrested, he initially denied deliberately using child sexual abuse material, but this was inconsistent with forensic evidence. David was found guilty at court and sentenced to imprisonment, which he later described as "the worst day of my life and yet the best day" because he tentatively began to talk to Emma for the first time about his thoughts and feelings and she stood by him during his period of imprisonment.

Out in the community, he had continuing difficulty taking about his offending and how to avoid relapsing but, with the support of his wife and probation officer, he began seeing a therapist who undertook so-called third wave psychological therapy, which includes helping people understand how their feelings of shame can stand in the way of dealing with their problems. It also helped him link some of his emotional difficulties to his early life experiences. Gradually David was able to access, own and appropriately share his thoughts and feelings with trusted others. David and Emma, now 32, have two small children and he has remained offence free over the last five years.

Fig. 2.2 Case example: David

compared to their subjective impressions prior to the pandemic. Furthermore, participants reported concerns for mental health, many of whom indicated increased symptoms of depression, anxiety, and loneliness.

Due to the travel restrictions related to the pandemic, (potential) travelling sex offenders were assumed to have engaged in increased online child sexual exploitation for their sexual gratification (INTERPOL, 2020). INTERPOL (2020) expected that more offenders might travel after restrictions were lifted, for example to commit hands-on abuse on children they exploited online during the pandemic.

More research is needed to understand the impact of the COVID-19 pandemic on the availability, distribution, and production of CSEM and the consequences for victims and perpetrators, including the hypothesised increased prevalence of international contact offending after travel restrictions were lifted.

Assessment of Risk and Need

A major concern of those working with CSEM offending—law enforcement, offender treatment services, and researchers—is that of risk assessment and management (including treatment interventions). The high and increasing level of CSEM offending requires decisions to be made about appropriate interventions for differential risk levels for this group of offenders. Use of interventions that do not conform to the well-established risk-need-responsivity principles (Andrews et al., 1990)—i.e., interventions should be directed at criminogenic needs and should be proportional to the risk level of the offending—are likely to be ineffectiveness or at worst counterproductive (Babchishin et al., 2018). For example, lengthy or intense interventions for individuals with low risks of reoffending could create an unnecessary dependence on therapy, inappropriately reinforcing the idea of higher risk than is the case and hindering the individual's development of self-efficacy and resilience.

Two large studies exploring the rates of previous convictions in men convicted of CSEM offending and three follow-up studies highlighted the relatively low association of CSEM offending with previous and subsequent contact offending in follow-ups ranging from 1 to 9 years, as illustrated in Tables 1 and 2.

Babchishin et al. (2011, 2015) conducted two meta-analyses of the profiles of, and reoffending by those (i) convicted of CSEM offences, (ii) contact sex offences against children and (iii) both (i.e., both contact and CSEM offending). They reported that, whilst CSEM offenders as a group displayed relatively higher sexual interest in children, as did the mixed offenders, they were unique in displaying low general antisociality. Their meta-analyses also highlighted the importance of the opportunity to offend, as the group who had engaged in contact offending reported more access to children in their lives compared to the group who had engaged in online offending.

As with risk assessments and intervention planning in other areas of forensic practice, it is important to combine actuarial assessments (i.e., predictions based on statistical modelling) with an individualised offence formulation (i.e., best working hypothesis of factors leading to offending based on the currently available evidence). These should ideally comprise a full history, functional analysis of the offending behaviour and use of structured professional judgement tools and relevant psychometric and other tests as appropriate. To date, the Child Pornography Offender Risk Tool (CPORT; Seto & Eke, 2015) is the only actuarial risk assessment tool specifically designed to assess recidivism risk in CSEM offenders. This tool has been shown to predict sexual recidivism in adult male CSEM offenders, albeit at a weaker level than similar tools for contact offenders (Eke et al., 2019).

One of the key factors in the CPORT is pedophilic interest, information on which may not be readily available. To address this, the CASIC (Correlates of Sexual Interest in Children) Scale was developed. This is an actuarially based tool developed as a proxy for paedophilic (prepubescent) and hebephilic (pubescent) sexual interest. It is scored on a total of six online and offline indicators as follows: a) child pornography including child sexual abuse videos, b) evidence of interest in child pornography for 2 + years, c) never married, d) child pornography included sex stories involving children, e) engaged in online sexual communication with a minor or officer posing as a minor, f) volunteered in a role with high access to children.

To complement actuarial risk assessments, Merdian and Perkins (2022) developed the Child Sexual Exploitation Material Pathways Tool (CPT) for case formulation with CSEM offenders to guide the design of appropriate interventions. The CPT was developed to fill a gap in resources for those working with this client group in order to, first, be a framework for collaborative exploration towards individualised case formulation; second, to complement other information on offence risk assessment, treatment needs, mental health issues etc.; and, third, to generate strategies for offence desistence and the development of a satisfying and offence-free future.

International Approaches to Tackling CSEM Offending

Interventions for CSEM offending risk fall broadly under the headings of tertiary, secondary, and primary prevention (Smallbone et al., 2013). Tertiary prevention is intervening with individuals who have already offended; secondary prevention involves identifying and intervening with individuals assessed as being at risk of offending, taking care to avoid stigmatisation and withdrawal from help (McCartan et al., 2018); and primary prevention comprises a range interventions applied across the population aimed at preventing offending occurring by tackling its underlying causes, for example adverse early life experiences, mental health issues and cultural and environmental factors.

In a review of treatment interventions for perpetrators of online child sexual abuse and exploitation, Perkins et al. (2018) identified 48 services or agencies providing interventions themselves, commissioning or conducting relevant research, and providing knowledge exchange events for professionals. This included eight UK-based services that directly provided interventions for perpetrators of online child sexual abuse and exploitation. These ranged from one-to one sessions to manualised treatment groups. They noted that little was known about the effectiveness of existing interventions, and whether there are gaps in the current intervention response. Interventions were limited and similar in their client focus, scope, and funding. They were predominantly psychoeducational, addressing psychological markers of offending behaviour, provided for men known to the criminal justice system, and are paid for by the client or as part of court-ordered or mandatory interventions.

Perkins et al. review identified the need for a shift towards preventative approaches—to increase public awareness and targeted at young people through educational resources. Sex education, including internet safety and pornography use, was highlighted by professionals as needing to be an integral part of the school curriculum, as was the implications of providing interventions for perpetrators not known to the criminal justice system, and for non-offending individuals who may be concerned about their sexual interest.

In the UK, the Lucy Faithfull Foundation is a charity dedicated to preventing child sexual abuse through its range of online and in-person psycho-educational and clinical services. It runs the Stop It Now UK & Ireland helpline, supporting anyone with concerns about child sexual abuse (Lucy Faithfull Foundation, 2022). The largest group that is being supported are people affected by online child sexual offending, most commonly the use of CSEM. They additionally provide psychoeducational programmes in the community that have shown positive results in evaluations (Dervley et al., 2017; Gillespie et al., 2018). These in-person groups ('Inform Plus) run over 10 sessions and cover: (a) offence analysis, (b) the role of sexual fantasy, (c) addictions and compulsions, (d) disclosure, relationships and social skills, (e) criminal justice information, (f) the impact of offending and (g) positive lifestyle change and safe future planning. Gillespie et al. (2018) reported positive changes at 8–10 week follow-up in Inform Plus participants' emotional and interpersonal functioning together with reductions in distorted attitudes about CSEM. A complementary qualitative evaluation of Inform Plus (Dervley et al., 2017) reported positive changes within participants on: (a) empowering self as an agent of change, (b) improvements in open communication, and (c) coming to understand that they could achieve a good life for themselves after treatment, many of which were also reported by participants' partners and the group facilitators.

Complementing this community support, the LFF 'Get Help' website provides further anonymous help for those at risk of CSEM offending. An independent evaluation of the Stop it Now! UK and Ireland Helpline (Brown et al., 2014), which provided support and guidance to prevent child sexual abuse through a free telephone and email service for over 31,000 calls received between 2002 and 2013 from potential abusers (8%) and those who had committed offences (48%), found it to be 'overwhelmingly positive' in demonstrating positive impacts, including helping users recognise problematic behaviours, implement prevention strategies, and improve well-being.

In Germany, which does not have mandatory reporting laws for specific professional groups that many other countries have, the Prevention Project Dunkelfeld (PPD) has offered preventative treatment for people with paedophilia and hebephilia, free of charge, since 2005 (Beier et al., 2009). The majority of PPD clients have engaged in CSEM offending (Beier et al., 2015). The PPD offers cognitive-behavioural group therapy that is based on sexual offending treatment programmes and focuses on the acceptance of the sexual interest, development of coping strategies, checking of any offence-supportive thinking styles, and strengthening of positive relationships (Beier, 2018). If clients wish, they may also receive medication that can help reduce sexual urges (Amelung et al., 2012). A first evaluation (Beier et al., 2015) has shown mixed results, with the most positive changes seen in clients who had engaged in hands-on and CSEM offending, followed by clients who had engaged in hands-on offending, and less change observed in those who had solely engaged in CSEM offences. No change in dynamic risk factors was observed in clients who had not committed any child sexual offences. A recent follow-up study (Beier et al., 2024) found that 89% of those PPD clients who had reported CSEM use before starting therapy had reoffended with CSEM, albeit with less 'severe' material. This indicates that the treatment needs of CSEM users and 'what works' with this group needs to be understood better.

Similar projects, aiming at the prevention of offending by people who have a sexual interest in children, have increasingly been implemented in other countries. An overview of support available per country for people with a sexual interest in children can be found at: https://helplinks.eu/.

The UK Government's'Tackling Child Sexual Abuse Strategy 2021', which covers all forms of child sexual abuse, sets out the need for an integrated approach to tackling offending and supporting all victims and survivors by (a) identifying more abuse and safeguarding more children through police recorded crime, children's social care data and independent inspectorate reports; (b) bringing more offenders to justice and increasing effective trials for child sexual abuse, based on data from across the criminal justice system; and (c) improving the quality and availability of support for victims and survivors, drawing on insight from delivery and third sector partners.

The UK Online Harms Bill, which has, at the time of writing, completed its passage through Parliament, includes in its requirements to (a) remove illegal content quickly or prevent it from appearing in the first place, including content promoting self-harm, (b) prevent children from accessing harmful and age-inappropriate content including pornographic content, (c) enforce age limits and use age-checking measures on platforms where content harmful to children is published, (d) ensure social media platforms are more transparent about the risks and dangers posed to children on their sites, including by publishing risk assessments, and

(e) provide parents and children with clear and accessible ways to report problems online when they do arise.

Technological Solutions

Considering that the use of legal adult pornography and problematic use of such material have repeatedly been identified as precursors to CSEM use (Bailey et al., 2022; Dreyhaupt, 2020), targeting platforms that host adult pornography may be a viable early intervention and deterrence of escalating behaviours. Warning messages have been shown effective in disrupting the use of 'barely legal' material (Prichard et al., 2022). Chatbots may also be used to deter escalating online behaviours (Prichard et al., 2022) and thereby prevent online sexual exploitation of more children.

To raise awareness of live streaming offences and detect offenders who exploit children via webcams, the non-governmental organisation Terre des Homme created a life-like artificial intelligence (AI) avatar of a young girl from the Philippines they called 'Sweetie' (Schermer et al., 2019). When "Sweetie" posed in various chatrooms in 2013, she was approached by over 20,000 men from over 70 countries over a period of ten weeks (Salinari, 2014). Interactions with these men allowed collection of intelligence that led to the identification of 1,000 men who engaged in sexual conversations with the avatar (Kleijn & Bogaerts, 2019). A chatbot in a popular adult pornography website has recently been found to reduce the searches for child-related material and stopped users in 82% of time periods spent on the website, from searching for child-related material again after getting connected with the chatbot (Smith, 2024). The chatbot popped up when users of the adult pornography website used search terms indicative of CSEM, and then directed them to support services. Such AI chatbots may therefore prove useful in detecting online offenders and deterring CSEM offending.

Conclusions

Child sexual exploitation material (CSEM) offending is increasing rapidly. It includes indecent images of children (IIOC) as well as written narratives. Those convicted of solely online CSEM offences tend to have lower recidivism rates and lower general antisociality compared to contact offenders. Only a small percentage of CSEM offenders go on to commit contact offences against children. This has implications for risk management and intervention approaches. CSEM serves various functions for offenders, for example sexual gratification, trading with others, financial gain and blackmail. Offenders often have early life experiences or psychological issues that contribute to their offences. Risk assessment tools like CPORT and CASIC can help gauge risk levels. Interventions for CSEM offenders vary and more research is needed on their effectiveness. They are mostly psychoeducational group therapies focused on psychological factors underlying offences. Live streaming of child abuse is an emerging threat, often involving offenders in wealthy countries exploiting vulnerable children in poorer countries. The COVID-19 lockdowns likely increased online sexual exploitation risks and offences. Strategies to tackle CSEM offending include improving detection, bringing more offenders to justice, supporting victims, regulating online platforms, and offering preventative therapy. Technological solutions like AI chatbots show promise for detecting and deterring online child exploitation.

Table 2.1 Rates of previous contact offending in CSEM users

	Previous convictions for contact sexual offending (mostly against children) (%)	*Self-reported previous contact offending (%)*
Hanson and Babchishin (2009; *n* = 3,536)	13.3	18.5
Seto et al., (2011; *n* = 4,697)	12.2	17.3

Table 2.2 Reconviction rates of CSEM users

	Follow-up period	*Reconviction for CSEM offending*	*Reconviction for contact offending*
Seto et al., (2011; *n* = 2,630)	1½–6-year follow-up	3.4%	2%
Faust et al., (2015 *n* = 638)	1–9-year follow-up	1.6%	3%
Elliott et al., (2019; *n* = 584)	After completion of community intervention; average follow-up: 13 years	7.4% in those who had only a conviction for CSEM	2.6% in those who had only a conviction for CSEM 9.4% in those who had an additional conviction for contact offending

References

Açar, K. V. (2017). Child abuse materials as digital goods: Why we should fear new commercial forms. *Economics Discussion Papers, 15*, 1–17.

Amelung, T., Kuhle, L. F., Konrad, A., Pauls, A., & Beier, K. M. (2012). Androgen deprivation therapy of self-identifying, help-seeking pedophiles in the Dunkelfeld. *International Journal of Law and Psychiatry, 35*(3), 176–184. https://doi.org/10.1016/j.ijlp.2012.02.005

Andrews, D. A., Bonta, J., & Hoge, R. D. (1990). Classification for effective rehabilitation: Rediscovering psychology. *Criminal Justice and Behavior, 17*, 19–52.

Babchishin, K. M., Hanson, R. K., & VanZuylen, H. (2015). Online child pornography offenders are different: A meta-analysis of the characteristics of online and offline sex offenders against children. *Archives of Sexual Behavior, 44*, 45–66. https://doi.org/10.1007/s10508-014-0270-x

Babchishin, K. M., Karl Hanson, R., & Hermann, C. A. (2011). The characteristics of online sex offenders: A metaanalysis. *Sexual Abuse, 23*(1), 92–123.

Babchishin, K. M., Merdian, H. L., Bartels, R. M., & Perkins, D. E. (2018). Child sexual exploitation materials offenders: A review. *European Psychologist, 23*(2), 130–143. https://doi.org/10.1027/1016-9040/a000326

Bailey, A., Allen, L., Stevens, E., Dervley, R., Findlater, D., & Wefers, S. (2022). Pathways and prevention for indecent images of children offending: A qualitative study. *Sexual Offending: Theory, Research, and Prevention, 17*, 1–24.

Bartels, R. M., & Merdian, H. L. (2016). The implicit theories of child sexual exploitation material users: An initial conceptualization. *Aggression and Violent Behavior, 26*, 16–25. https://doi.org/10.1016/j.avb.2015.11.002

Beier, K. M. (2018). BEDIT-Manual für Erwachsene. In K. M. Beier (Ed.), *Pädophilie, Hebephilie und sexueller Kindesmissbrauch* (pp. 59–68). Springer. https://doi.org/10.1007/978-3-662-56594-0_5

Beier, K. M., Grundmann, D., Kuhle, L. F., Scherner, G., Konrad, A., & Amelung, T. (2015). The German Dunkelfeld Project: A pilot study to prevent child sexual abuse and the use of child abusive images. *The Journal of Sexual Medicine, 12*(2), 529–542. https://doi.org/10.1111/jsm.12785

Beier, K. M., Nentzl, J., von Heyden, M., Fishere, M., & Amelung, T. (2024). Preventing child sexual abuse and the use of child sexual abuse material: Following up on the German Prevention Project Dunkelfeld. *Journal of Prevention*. https://doi.org/10.1007/s10935-024-00792-0

Beier, K. M., Neutze, J., Mundt, I. A., Ahlers, C. J., Goecker, D., Konrad, A., & Schaefer, G. A. (2009). Encouraging self-identified pedophiles and hebephiles to seek professional help: First results of the Prevention Project Dunkelfeld (PPD). *Child Abuse & Neglect, 33*(8), 545–549. https://doi.org/10.1016/j.chiabu.2009.04.002

Brown, A., Jago, N., Kerr, J., McNaughton Nicholls, C., Paskell, C., & Webster, S. (2014). Call to keep children safe from sexual abuse: A study of the use and effects of the Stop it Now! UK and Ireland helpline. NatCen Social Research. https://www.stopitnow.org.uk/wp-content/uploads/2020/01/stop_it_now_evaluation_uk_findings.pdf

Brown, R., Napier, S., & Smith, R. G. (2020). Australians who view live streaming of child sexual abuse: An analysis of financial transactions. *Trends & Issues in Crime and Criminal Justice, 589*, 1–16.

Christensen, L. S., & Woods, J. (2024). It's Like POOF and It's Gone: The Live-Streaming of Child Sexual Abuse. *Sexuality & Culture, 28*(4), 1467–1481.

Council of Europe. (2007). *Council of Europe Convention on the Protection of Children against Sexual Exploitation and Sexual Abuse. Lanzarote, 25.X.2007*. Council of Europe. Retrieved from https://rm.coe.int/1680084822

Cubitt, T. I. C., Napier, S., & Brown, R. (2023). Understanding the offline criminal behavior of individuals who live stream child sexual abuse. *Journal of*

Interpersonal Violence, 38(9–10), 6624–6649. https://doi.org/10.1177/08862605221137712
de Tribolet-Hardy, F., Hill, A., & Habermeyer, E. (2020). Webcam child sexual abuse: Eine neue Facette der Begutachtung von Internetsexualdelinquenz. *Forensische Psychiatrie, Psychologie, Kriminologie, 14*, 259–269. https://doi.org/10.1007/s11757-020-00613-0
Dervley, R., Perkins, D., Whitehead, H., Bailey, A., Gillespie, S., & Squire, T. (2017). Themes in participant feedback on risk reduction programme for child sexual exploitation material offenders. *Journal of Sexual Aggression, 23*(1), 46–61. https://doi.org/10.1080/13552600.2016.1269958
Dreyhaupt, R. (2020). It took me down a rabbit hole: Onset and maintenance factors of child sexual exploitation material offending behaviour (Unpublished master's thesis). Maastricht University.
ECPAT. (2017). *Online child sexual exploitation: A common understanding*. ECPAT International.
ECPAT. (2020, April 7). Why children are at risk of sexual abuse and exploitation during COVID-19. https://ecpat.org/story/why-children-are-at-risk-of-sexual-exploitation-during-covid-19/
ECPAT. (n.d.). Global progress towards ending the sexual exploitation of children. Available at: https://ecpat.org/our-impact/
Eke, A. W., Helmus, L. M., & Seto, M. C. (2019). A validation study of the child pornography offender risk tool (CPORT). *Sexual Abuse, 31*(4), 456–476.
Elliott, I. A., Mandeville-Norden, R., Rakestrow-Dickens, J., & Beech, A. R. (2019). Reoffending rates in a UK community sample of individuals with convictions for indecent images of children. *Law and Human Behavior, 43* 4), 369–382. https://doi.org/10.1037/lhb0000328
EUROPOL. (2016). *Internet organised crime threat assessment*. Europol.
EUROPOL. (2020). Covid-19: Child sexual exploitation. Retrieved from https://www.europol.europa.eu/covid-19/covid-19-child-sexual-exploitation
EUROPOL. (2021, December 6). Exploiting isolation: Offenders and victims of online child sexual abuse during the COVID-19 pandemic. https://www.europol.europa.eu/publications-documents/exploiting-isolation-offenders-and-victims-of-online-child-sexual-abuse-during-covid-19-pandemic
Faust, E., Bickart, W., Renaud, C., & Camp, S. (2015). Child pornography possessors and child contact sex offenders: A multilevel comparison of demographic characteristics and rates of recidivism. *Sexual Abuse, 27*(5), 460–478.
Gillespie, S. M., Bailey, A., Squire, T., Carey, M. L., Eldridge, H. J., & Beech, A. R. (2018). An evaluation of a community-based psycho-educational program for users of child sexual exploitation material. *Sexual Abuse, 30*(2), 169–191.
Hackett, S., Branigan, P., & Holmes, D. (2019). *Operational framework for children and young people displaying harmful sexual behaviours*. NSPCC.

https://www.icmec.org/wp-content/uploads/2019/04/harmful-sexual-behaviour-framework.pdf
Hanson, R. K., & Babchishin, K. M. (2009, April). How should we advance our knowledge of risk assessment for internet sex offenders. In *Global Symposium for Examining the Relationship between Online and Offline Offences and Preventing the Sexual Exploitation of Children, University of North Carolina, Chapel Hill, NC*.
Internet Watch Foundation. (2022, February 8). Call for lawmakers to act quickly as new data shows child sexual abuse reports are soaring in wake of pandemic. https://www.iwf.org.uk/news-media/news/call-for-lawmakers-to-act-quickly-as-new-data-shows-child-sexual-abuse-reports-are-soaring-in-wake-of-pandemic/
Internet Watch Foundation. (2023, October 25). 'Worst nightmares' come true as predators are able to make thousands of new AI images of real child victims. Retrieved from https://www.iwf.org.uk/news-media/news/worst-nightmares-come-true-as-predators-are-able-to-make-thousands-of-new-ai-images-of-real-child-victims/
Internet Watch Foundation. (2024). *IWF annual report 2023*. Retrieved from https://www.iwf.org.uk/annual-report-2023/
INTERPOL. (2020, September). Threats and trends: Child sexual exploitation and abuse - COVID-19 impact.
Kemp, S., Buil-Gil, D., Moneva, A., Miro-Llinares, F., & Diaz-Castano, N. (2021). Empty streets, busy internet: A time-series analysis of cybercrime and fraud trends during COVID-19. *Journal of Contemporary Criminal Justice, 37*(4), 480–501. https://doi.org/10.1177/10439862211027986
Kleijn, M., & Bogaerts, S. (2019). Sexual-oriented online chat conversations: Characteristics and testing pathways of online perpetrators. In S. van der Hof, I. Georgieva, B. Schermer, & B. Koops (Eds.), *Sweetie 2.0: Using artificial intelligence to fight webcam child sex tourism* (pp. 95–112). Asser Press. https://doi.org/10.1007/978-94-6265-288-0
Kuhlmann, D. F., & Auren, S. (2015). Nipa huts with high-speed internet: Commercial exploitation of children in the 21st century - A qualitative investigation of webcam child prostitution in the Philippines (Master's thesis). Lund University.
Liggett, R., Lee, J. R., Roddy, A. L., & Wallin, M. A. (2020). The dark web as a platform for crime: An exploration of illicit drug, firearm, CSAM, and cybercrime markets. In T. J. Holt & A. M. Bossler (Eds.), *The Palgrave handbook of international cybercrime and cyberdeviance* (pp. 91–116). https://doi.org/10.1007/978-3-319-78440-3_17
Lucy Faithfull Foundation. (2022). *Annual report and financial statement 2021/22*. Retrieved from https://www.lucyfaithfull.org.uk/files/LFF_Annual_Report_2021-22_FINAL.pdf

McCartan, K. F., Merdian, H. L., Perkins, D. E., & Kettleborough, D. (2018). Ethics and issues of secondary prevention efforts in child sexual abuse. *International Journal of Offender Therapy and Comparative Criminology, 62*(9), 2548–2566. https://doi.org/10.1177/0306624X17723951

McMahan, A., Roche, K., Dreyhaupt, R., Seto, M. C., & Rahm, C. (2023). Changes in sexual thoughts and behaviors in a clinical sample of child sexual abuse material users under the COVID-19 pandemic. *Sexual and Relationship Therapy*. https://doi.org/10.1080/14681994.2023.2215710

Merdian, H. L., & Perkins, D. E. (2022). Working with individuals who have accessed child sexual exploitation material: Assessment strategies and future developments. In *Challenges in the management of people convicted of a sexual offence: A way forward* (pp. 85–101).

Merdian, H. L., Curtis, C., Thakker, J., Wilson, N., & Boer, D. P. (2013a). The three dimensions of online child pornography offending. *Journal of Sexual Aggression, 19*(1), 121–132. https://doi.org/10.1080/13552600.2011.611898

Merdian, H. L., Perkins, D., McCashin, D., & Stevanovic, J. (2020). Integrating structured individual offending pathway analysis into group treatment for individuals who have accessed, shared, and/or distributed child sexual exploitation material: A feasibility study and preliminary outcome evaluation. *Psychology, Crime & Law, 27*(6), 579–605. https://doi.org/10.1080/1068316X.2020.1849690

Merdian, H. L., Wilson, N., Thakker, J., Curtis, C., & Boer, D. P. (2013b). So why did you do it?": Explanations provided by child pornography offenders. *Sexual Offender Treatment, 8*(1), 1–19.

Merdian, H., Perkins, D., Dustagheer, E., & Glorney, E. (2018). Development of a case formulation model for users of child sexual exploitation material. *International Journal of Offender Therapy and Comparative Criminology, 64*(10–11), 1055–1073. https://doi.org/10.1177/0306624X17748067

Middleton, D., Elliott, I., Mandeville-Norden, R., & Beech, A. (2006). An investigation into the applicability of the Ward and Siegert pathways model of child sexual abuse with Internet offenders. *Psychology, Crime & Law, 12*(6), 589–603.

Munns, N., Brennan, M., Byrnes, E., Sheridan, C., Jabar, M., Tarroja, M., Collado, Z., & Perkins, D. (2024). *Facilitation of online sexual abuse and exploitation of children (OSAEC) in the Philippines.* Justice & Care.

Naldrett, G., Simonet, R., & Findlater, D. (2021). *An initial analysis of the impact of the coronavirus pandemic on callers to the Stop It Now! UK and Ireland helpline.* Lucy Faithfull Foundation. https://www.stopitnow.org.uk/wp-content/uploads/2021/10/Covid_19_insights_from_the_Stop_It_Now_helpline_summary_April-September_2020.pdf

National Crime Agency. (2019). *National strategic assessment of serious and organised crime*. National Crime Agency.
National Crime Agency. (2023). *National strategic assessment for serious and organised crime*. National Crime Agency. https://www.nationalcrimeagency.gov.uk/images/NSA_2023_Website_-_PDF_Version_1.pdf
Perkins, D., Merdian, H., Schumacher, B., Bradshaw, H., & Stevanovic, J. (2018). Interventions for perpetrators of online child sexual exploitation: A scoping review and gap analysis. Centre of Expertise on Child Sexual Abuse: Child sexual exploitation perpetrators research programme, Report 5.
Prichard, J., Scanlan, J., Watters, P., Wortley, R., Hunn, C., & Garrett, E. (2022). *Online messages to reduce users' engagement with child sexual abuse material: A review of relevant literature for the rethink Chatbot*. University of Tasmania.
Pritchard, J., Wortley, R., Watters, P. A., Spiranovic, C., Hunn, C., & Krone, T. (2022). Effects of automated messages on internet users attempting to access "barely legal" pornography. *Sexual Abuse, 34*(1), 106–124. https://doi.org/10.1177/10790632211013809
Protect Children. (2024, February). *Tech platforms used by online child sexual abuse offenders: Research report with actionable recommendations for the tech industry*. Suojellan Lapsia, Protect Children ry.
Ramiro, L. S., Martinez, A. B., Tan, J. R. D., Mariano, K., Miranda, G. M. J., & Bautista, G. (2019). Online child sexual exploitation and abuse: A community diagnosis using the social norms theory. *Child Abuse & Neglect, 96*, Article 104080. https://doi.org/10.1016/j.chiabu.2019.104080
Roser, M., Ritchie, H., & Ortiz-Ospina, E. (2015). Our world in data - Internet. Retrieved from https://ourworldindata.org/internet#citation
Salinari, R. K. (2014). Webcam child sex tourism: Stopping the growing number of predators. *Freedom from Fear, 9*, 72–77. https://doi.org/10.18356/8e294485-en
Schermer, B., Georgieva, I., van der Hof, S., & Koops, B. (2019). Legal aspects of sweetie 2.0. In S. van der Hof, I. Georgieva, B. Schermer, & B. Koops (Eds.), *Sweetie 2.0: Using artificial intelligence to fight webcam child sex tourism* (pp. 1–94). Asser Press. https://doi.org/10.1007/978-94-6265-288-0
Seto, M. C., & Eke, A. W. (2015). Predicting recidivism among adult male child pornography offenders: Development of the Child Pornography Offender Risk Tool (CPORT). *Law and Human Behavior, 39*(4), 416–429. https://doi.org/10.1037/lhb0000128
Seto, M. C., Karl Hanson, R., & Babchishin, K. M. (2011). Contact sexual offending by men with online sexual offenses. *Sexual Abuse, 23*(1), 124–145. https://doi.org/10.1177/1079063210369013

Skidmore, M., Aitkenhead, B. & Muir, R. (2022). Turning the tide against online child sexual abuse. The Police Foundation. https://www.police-foundation.org.uk/wp-content/uploads/2022/07/turning_the_tide_FINAL-.pdf

Smallbone, S., Marshall, W. L., & Wortley, R. (2013). Preventing child sexual abuse: Evidence, policy and practice. *Willan*. https://doi.org/10.4324/9781843925606

Smith, S. (2024). Chatbots and warning messages: Innovations in the fight against online child sexual abuse. *Faithfull Paper*. https://www.lucyfaithfull.org.uk/files/Faithfull_Paper_Chatbots_12_Sept_2024.pdf

UNICEF. (2020). COVID-19 and its implications for protecting children online. https://www.unicef.org/media/67396/fle/COVID-19%20and%20Its%20Implications%20for%20Protecting%20Children%20Online.pdf.

United Nations. (2000, May 25). *Optional protocol to the Convention on the Rights of the Child on the sale of children, child prostitution and child pornography*. Resolution A/RES/54/263 at the fifty-fourth session of the General Assembly of the United Nations. Retrieved from https://www.ohchr.org/en/instruments-mechanisms/instruments/optional-protocol-convention-rights-child-sale-children-child

Varella, A. (2017). Live streaming of child sexual abuse: Background, legislative frameworks and the experience of the Philippines. *ECPAT International Journal, 12*, 47–61.

Ward, T., & Siegert, R. J. (2002). Toward a comprehensive theory of child sexual abuse: A theory knitting perspective. *Psychology, crime and law, 8*(4), 319–351.

WePROTECT Global Alliance. (2019). *Global threat assessment 2019: Working together to end the sexual exploitation of children online*. WePROTECT Global Alliance.

CHAPTER 3

Blackmail and Sextortion

Ian Baker, Tadgh Tobin, Belinda Winder, Rebecca Lievesley, and Daria Kuss

Introduction

This chapter focuses on the sexual blackmail or coercion of children. Blackmail is typically seen as a marginal crime, falling outside daily policing and political priorities (Peelo & Soothill, 2014). Blackmail only achieves notoriety when serious cases capture public interest. In a study of over 50 years of blackmail convictions, there was a clear "ebb and flow"

I. Baker · T. Tobin · B. Winder (✉) · R. Lievesley · D. Kuss
Nottingham Trent University, Nottingham, England
e-mail: belinda.winder@ntu.ac.uk

I. Baker
e-mail: ian.baker67@me.com

T. Tobin
e-mail: tadgh.tobin@ntu.ac.uk

R. Lievesley
e-mail: rebecca.lievesley@ntu.ac.uk

D. Kuss
e-mail: daria.kuss@ntu.ac.uk

C. A. Harper et al. (eds.), *Sexual Crime and the Internet*, Sexual Crime,
https://doi.org/10.1007/978-3-031-95844-1_3

(Peelo & Soothill, 2014, p. 234) of the reporting of cases, depending on moral panics of the time. Thus, the popular ***modus operandi*** of blackmail convictions shows a tendency to gently morph with time, dependent on the current social anxieties, be they police corruption or gang violence (1970s), trade union activity (1980s), or consumer terrorism (1990s). We could add here the moral panic about sexual crimes in the last 20 years to these.

People who commit blackmail distort reality in their favour to oblige a victim to comply with their demands. They create a sense of low self-esteem or interpersonal dependency to make victims comply with demands (Forward & Frazier, 1996). Manipulation utilises a victim's fear, obligation, or guilt to manipulate the victim into complying with a demand (Forward & Frazier, 1996). Blackmail creates an offence by threatening to carry out actions that may not ordinarily be a crime. The disclosure of information may not be a criminal offence, but if an individual were to ask for a sum of money to ***not*** disclose this information it creates the offence of blackmail (Robinson et al., 2010). Blackmail, coercion, or extortion all sit on liminal places; they have similar definitions and involve similar actions. Sometimes these actions are criminal, and sometimes not, the boundary of which can often be contextual (Robinson et al., 2010). Theories suggest that changes in the power base of a relationship can change the interaction into a criminal offence. These changes range from a moral improperness of actions to the creation of "relationship of dominance and subordination between the blackmailer and recipient" (Robinson et al., 2010, p. 299).

The success of blackmail depends upon the vulnerability the victim feels. These vulnerabilities may take the form of the fear of losing self-respect, self-worth, reputation, or of relationship breakdown, among others. If that vulnerability can be removed, the success of blackmail can be limited (Altman, 1993). Victim selection in child sexual abuse can be based on perceived vulnerability (Conte et al., 1989). Pre-internet research found that people convicted of sexual abuse used statements such as "has a look of being vulnerable in some way", or "I would pick the one who appeared more needy" when describing victim targeting (Conte et al., 1989, p. 296). The risk of online solicitation was higher for those children categorised as "troubled" or using internet behaviour that increased risk (Finkelhor et al., 2000). In the case of online sexual coercion of children, it is possibly the vulnerabilities as highlighted by Conte et al. (1989) and Finkelhor et al. (2000) that are noticed and exploited. For blackmail/coercion to be successful, a person needs to be able to provide a leverage or means to force the victim to pursue a course of action. This can range from a subtle coercive request which a victim complies with to gain acceptance or maintain a friendship, to a more forceful request in the form of blackmail with a direct threat to enforce compliance. While it can be argued that one is more forceful than the other, the subsequent outcome can be just as serious whichever method is used.

The use of coercive tactics or blackmail within sexual offending is sometimes an intrinsic part of the grooming process. Around half of all people with sexual convictions against children used intimidation or threats in committing contact offences (Lang & Frenzel, 1988). In a study of 250 children, over half were coerced into sexual acts (Defrancis, 1969). The age of this last reference suggests coercion is a long standing and established method of gaining compliance from child victims of sexual abuse. The participants of research into pre-internet contact offences indicated that they would use a variety of methods to trick, bribe or coerce children to seduction, these would be followed up with warnings used to maintain secrecy (Lang & Frenzel, 1988). Although these assumptions are pre-internet, the manipulation, power, and control over victims seem to form important factors in the commission of the Internet-based crimes. But there can also be more subtle drivers, including a need of power, affiliation or achievement. Those with a higher need for power are more likely to select the power bases of impersonal coercion or legitimate position to achieve their goals (Raven, 2008).

Online Sexual Coercion Against Children—Sextortion

Sextortion is often used as an all-encompassing term to describe online sexual extortion. It is described by as "the threatened dissemination of explicit, intimate, or embarrassing images of a sexual nature without consent, usually for the purpose of procuring additional images, sexual acts, money or something else" (Patchin & Hinduja, 2018, p. 140). Sextortion is a very loose term which covers a multitude of scenarios, against both children and adults, and falls under the category of "image based sexual abuse" (Henry et al., 2018, p. 566) as a form of "technology facilitated sexual violence" (2018, p. 565). People who commit Sextortion offences can inflict misery and suffering on their victims, forcing them to take part in increasingly demanding sex acts under threat of being publicly exposed to their friends and family (Wittes et al., 2016). Victims also have trouble in breaking the cycle of progressive online sexual coercion and abuse that develops (Wittes et al., 2016). Indeed, agencies such as Child Exploitation and Online Protection Centre (2010) and the FBI (2016) believe that the use of coercive tactics within sextortion demands against children is increasing. Sextortion demands against children often involve coercing the child to produce and share sexual images of themselves or friends, often to be shared or traded in online fora, increasing the reputation of the supplier (Europol, 2015).

Due to inconsistent definition and categorisation, incidence and prevalence data for online sexually coercive offences against children are difficult to obtain (Wittes et al., 2016), and previous studies have not always clearly differentiated between cyber-bullying and sextortion. However, a study conducted in the USA indicated that 5% of under 18 s have been subjected to sextortion, with a higher percentage of victims falling into the 13–17 age group (Patchin & Hinduja, 2018). Victimisation was found that to be more common among males (5.8%) than females (5.0%), and among non-heterosexual victims (10.9%) than heterosexual victims (4.5%; Patchin & Hinduja, 2018). The dichotomous nature of this study, as identified by the authors, made it difficult to understand some of the context behind the victim's experiences. Consequently, it is not known how frequently they occurred or the type of relationship the victim held with the person who is committing the offence. The majority (over 60%) of victims in the Patchin and Hinduja study personally knew their abuser. The representation of unknown cases involving exclusively online offending was relatively low. The research by Patchin and Hinduja (2018) did not examine the motivations of those who wished to commit online sexual coercion.

Committing Online Sexual Coercion

Kopecký (2017) stated that the online sexual blackmailing of children can have the following intentions:

1. To obtain money,
2. As a constituent part of a grooming offence with a view to meeting up with the child,

3. With the intent of obtaining intimate or indecent photographs or video footage of the child.

The third element—obtaining sexual imagery was referred to as sextortion (Kopecký, 2017). In this study of 1374 victims, 73% were female and 27% male, victim ages ranged from 11 to 17 years. The research carried out in partnership with cyber-crime specialists in the Czech Republic analysed the communications of both people who were convicted of the offence and their victims. It found that the ages of people who committed the offences ranged from 28 to 39 years old and presented that many of the cases would not have occurred if the victim took preventative actions to protect themselves. This was explained by concluding that in a non-virtual world people are taught "defense mechanisms" (Kopecký et al., 2014, p. 17) by being warned against risks by parents or teachers. It opined that risk management was not as common in the virtual world. The internet is viewed as a place where one can escape from reality, during leisure time and not have to worry about problems faced in the real world. As such, people discuss topics they normally would not or speak with less inhibition. Consequently, it is argued that an individual becomes more vulnerable to cyber-bullying, and ergo sextortion (Kopecký et al., 2014).

Reported methods to commit online sexual coercion vary. They have included cases utilising malware to remotely access webcams and locate personal information and files from potential victims, or more simply just asking victims for an initial image. The information or images are then used to coerce victims into creating sexual images and videos (Wittes et al., 2016). The knowledge that sexual images were obtained through fear, fraud and coercion and that there is no subsequent control over them has proven too devastating for some teenagers to deal with (Webster et al., 2012), sometimes leading to suicide.

There are three pre-conditions that need to be present for sextortion (Acar, 2016):

1. Cyberspace—interactions occur online,
2. Possession—the person initiating the offence needs to possess a sexual image, or other compromising material or information to shift the balance of power in their favour,
3. Extortion—once the person initiating the offence has the balance of power, demands can be made of the victim.

Prevention can be effective by removing or disrupting just one of these elements (Acar, 2016). The child (victim) is the initial holder of power in the online relationship until the person committing the offence acquires an image or some other piece of valuable information. At this point the child then becomes vulnerable and can be blackmailed. Analysing chat logs on social media forums, a 5-stage model to represent the process of online sexual blackmail of children was created (Kopecký, 2017):

1. Establish contact with child—often the contact would be represented as accidental, allowing chat to be established. Dependent on outcome, the aggressor may send non-intimate images.
2. Manipulation through compliments—positive or flattering comments are made about the victim.
3. Verification of victim's identity—attempts are made to confirm that the victim is a child and that they are willing to send real images.
4. Intimacy intensifying—the move from non-intimate to intimate images is made. Further requests may be made for the performance of sexual acts, photographs or videos. Naked or sexual photographs may be sent to the child by the person committing the offence.
5. Blackmail—if the child declines to exchange images blackmail may be used. Threats include revealing images to friends or family members.

In some cases, attempts are made to force the victim to meet in the physical world or to exploit the child financially (Kopecký, 2017). None of the children in the study who were targeted during the 2-to-3-month periods of victimisation advised parents/adults/carers, but some did use online help/report links (Kopecký, 2017). Once the person initiating a blackmail transaction obtains a sexual image by using coercive methods, the number of images obtained increased dramatically. Females in the age group of 15–17 are more likely to be targeted by blackmail, and those who have been blackmailed were more likely to use a similar tactic themselves (Kopecký, 2017). This subsequent use of blackmail was attributed to victims wishing to take revenge.

According to Acar "abusers rarely execute their threats and usually move to the next victim" (2016, p.120). This can increase the risk of detection by exposing the real identity of the person committing the offence, bringing them to the attention of law enforcement. With the execution of the threat reducing the power balance by sacrificing any images or knowledge that they hold. As they can victimise many children (Acar, 2016; Wittes et al., 2016), it is likely to be easier to move to another victim than to persist if one represents a risk. However, research into the childhood victimisation of now-adult participants (18-to-25-year-olds) found that nearly half of them reported the person who committed the offence acted on threats, publishing their sexual images (Wolak & Finkelhor, 2016). Further, victims showed a reluctance to tell anyone what they experienced, despite approximately 25% reporting the sextortion lasting over 6 months.

It was stated that those committing sextortion offences against children display similar traits to those committing sexual offences both on- and offline (O'Malley & Holt, 2020). A study of 152 people convicted of sexual offences found that they demonstrated higher levels of unhealthy sexual interests through their collections of child sexual abuse material, and coercion of children to abuse others. In sextortion offences, it is much less likely for the person convicted of the offence to know the victim, which is more common in contact offending (O'Malley & Holt, 2020). Additionally, power and control are often achieved through threats of distributing victim images, whereas in offline offending, power and control was achieved through different means, such as force or financial reward.

A further difference between online abuse and offline tactics is the remoteness and anonymity of the attacker and the unfamiliarity of parents/guardians with online communication methods (Dehue et al., 2008). The assailant is unable to witness the response of the victim to the attack, which can then result in an increasingly aggressive attack (Dehue et al., 2008, p. 217). This form of attack in what was is perceived as a safe environment—such as the family home, can have the tendency to increase its impact on the victim (Dehue et al., 2008). Black et al. (2015) opined that people committing online offences employ similar grooming strategies to those used by people committing offline offences including flattery and intimidation. These online strategies move at different speeds to suit the environment. For example, flattery and risk assessment strategies can be deployed immediately to try and assess whether the victim is indeed a genuine child or a police officer. Those committing online offences are able deploy grooming strategies allowing them to target and manage multiple victims at the same time in sextortion cases (Wittes et al., 2016).

Prosecuting Sexual Coercion of Children

Wittes et al. (2016) highlighted that the prosecutions of sextortion resulted in varied sentencing. However, in the UK, revised guidance on cases involving social media communication or internet-enabled abuse was originally issued in October 2013 but has been frequently updated (CPS, 2023). The existence of guidance suggests that a recognition of a need to standardise approaches to prosecution. It introduced categories against which prosecutors must assess online communications where a victim is subject to behaviour such as coercion, and blackmail. The varying categories allow the CPS to process cases appropriate to the severity. However, there was very little other guidance publicly available, and with no specific sextortion legislation, enforcement bodies have had to use other statutes to prosecute the crime. Because of this, cases are dealt with under a range of offences (Wittes et al., 2016) including indecent image or computer misuse laws. It is further claimed that sentencing for sextortion contains many irregularities within multi-victim cases. Examples are given where a person has offended against numerous victims and did not receive a higher penalty than those with fewer victims (Wittes et al., 2016). This highlights a lack of knowledge around sextortion, and suggests training is needed to support more consistent prosecutions across jurisdictions.

The visibility element of Sexual Extortion of Children in Cyberspace (SECC) is low; only a small number of cases are brought to justice and few victims are identified, with confusion over classification of incidents being partly responsible (Acar, 2016). Unclear and multiple definitions do not help in this respect, SECC could be considered as grooming under the definitions given by Krone (2004) but could also be categorised as cyber-bullying (Kopecký et al., 2014). This lack of consistency also extends into law enforcement (HMIC, 2016). Various motivations for engaging in sextortion of children can influence the crime classification process, for example financial exploitation would be different to generating indecent images of children (Acar, 2016).

Sextortion—Key Findings

The literature about the online sexual coercion of children is still developing, but there are findings that offer useful prevention strategies and guidance. Acar (2016) outlined the best method of prevention was to stop the circulation of compromising images in the first place, thus a refusal to comply with threats was a passive but effective method of prevention. The research provided by Kopecký (2014, 2017) has assisted the development of a prevention program in Czech schools, which raises awareness of and ways to mitigate risks to children on social networks, including verifying the identity of online contacts and maintaining privacy of information.

There has been a gradual progression towards a regulatory framework affording greater protection for children from exposure to online harms (Wright & Javid, 2020). The "Online Harms White Paper" (Wright & Javid, 2020) sought to put in place formal regulation of social media platform providers and "tech" companies—taking away the element of self-regulation currently relied upon. The Internet and technology have provided an ideal locus for sexual criminality against children (Taylor & Quayle, 2006). Studies suggest that children using social networking sites face higher levels of risks while online (Straksrud et al., 2013). Not using this knowledge to reduce the online risks faced by children suggests a failure to adequately mitigate them.

Sextortion is a crime that occurs when threats are made to an individual to force them to provide sexual images. Sextortion is "easy to accomplish" (Wittes et al., 2016, p. 3) and can target both adults and children alike. It can involve a range of actions from the theft of extant sexual images through hacking to encouraging the generation of new sexual images to be shared or used as leverage. Sextortion can be facilitated by any platform that allows messaging between users, but social media and gaming sites are particularly prevalent in this area (Europol, 2015). Initially, harmless conversations can develop into sexual ones, resulting in sextortion, with victims often being victimised within their own homes. Around 86% of sexual images of children aged 15 and under are created in the home environment, frequently in the bedroom or bathroom of the victim's home on a mobile phone (Europol, 2015). People who perpetrate sextortion often have multiple victims at a time, and it can be devastating to victims, with around 28% of cases resulting in suicidal behaviours (US Department of Justice, 2016; Wittes, 2016).

This chapter aimed to examine "how sextortion happens". It does this by utilising comparative case studies which present data from published criminal convictions to establish whether reported "real life" scenarios support the published research, and to provide direction for the further empirical studies of this thesis. While case studies are a method that are considered as appropriate for the exploratory phase of research, they can also provide causal explanation (see Goertz & Levy, 2007). Case studies can attract criticism for not being carried out with the rigour of traditional academic methods of research or being teaching cases as opposed to true research (Yin, 2018). However transparent, methodical and balanced results presentation avoids any potential research bias (Rosenthal & Rosnow, 2009) and provides balanced inference based on the evidence within the data.

Method

With the aim of exploring "how sextortion happens", data samples were obtained from cases reported in open-source documents. These included reports from police, courts, and news media. These are essentially sources of secondary data which present facts regarding real crime cases. The researcher has no control over the facts or content presented. It is recognised that contents could be factually limited and potentially affected by reporter bias, however, objective facts of the cases will not be skewed by such bias. The information is essential to fully understand a criminal phenomenon.

Data Collection

Data were collected by performing Internet searches using the keywords "sextortion", "sexual blackmail", "sexual coercion", and "sexual extortion". The searches were conducted between 2017 and 2018. It should be noted that the results of Internet searches change with time,[1] searches conducted during this research may be difficult to replicate. Searches were carried out using Google, Bing and the Nottingham Trent University library search engine. No geographical restrictions were applied to the case search, as literature indicated those committing sexual offences can cross international boundaries (Wittes, 2016). The searches output over 1200 sources for potential cases. To reduce this number, a three-stage process was applied to filter, include/exclude, and then select cases most relevant to the study. These cases were subject to the data extraction criteria to provide a specific standard of information to be studied. This

[1] https://www.nibusinessinfo.co.uk/content/what-search-engine-and-how-do-they-work.

process involved the manual examination of the source titles returned by each search engine. The criteria as outlined below were applied.

Filtering Out Criteria

1. Included within first four pages of results.
2. Sources from before 2000 were removed due to the infancy of the internet, and its lower level of use within a residential setting.
3. The case to be reported in English to avoid translation errors.
4. The search result had to report the conviction of person/s for a sexual offence against a victim under 18 years of age.

The intention of the filtering out process was to increase the relevancy of the cases in the search results and minimise the risk of translational error. At the conclusion of this stage, 87 potential cases remained.

Inclusion Criteria

Specific inclusion criteria were applied to the remaining cases they had to adhere to the following points:

1. Child victim—Cases where the victim ages were unclear were excluded.
2. Finalised prosecution—All sub-judicial or appeal-pending cases were excluded.
3. Contains direct evidence of coercion or threats were used to enforce demand for images/video.
4. Factual cases only—only news, court, or police reports were used or other, reliable and accountable sources.

With the range of one to six sources for each case, dependent on the popularity of online reporting, any duplicated cases were then aggregated, reducing the number of cases for consideration to 32.

Specific Selection Criteria

The third and final stage was the application of a set of specific criteria which had to be present for the case to be included in the comparative case analysis.

1. Communication between convicted person and victim occurred online.
2. The case had to include the victim being subject to a threat/coercion where sexual images/video were demanded.
3. The sexual images requested had to be of a child.

No restriction was placed on the type of electronic device used in the offence. Nor did the victim and convicted person need to be in the same country when the offending occurred.

A total of 21 separate prosecution cases remained after the three-stage process, all of which were included in this comparative case study. One included case had two defendants, which are reported separately hereafter, therefore the following sections discuss $n = 22$ people who were convicted.

Verification

All selected cases were checked for accuracy. This was accomplished by conducting additional Internet searches using the available names of the convicted person/s. Additional searches were also included the terms "sex", "conviction", "online", "internet", "offence", and "offender", "child porn" in conjunction with the name/s given in the selected cases. The intent was to remove cases with contradictory/inconsistent information, however this was not necessary, as there were no pertinent inconsistencies.

Procedure

The data used in this study came from numerous different sources. To standardise the information within each of the individual cases, the factual data were listed in a spreadsheet and placed into data fields. If information was unclear, it was omitted to avoid misrepresentation. The data fields containing similar facts, such as number of victims, ages, sentencing, and *modus operandi* were clustered together. Any data field that was not populated by at least 70% of the cases was subsequently omitted, subsequently, 31 key evaluation data fields remained. Where data fields were text-based, standardised words and phrases were used for example, where possible, phrases such as "posed as teenage female", or "befriended teenagers on social media" would be used to enable comparison. If the original author's opinion was presented within a report, this was omitted.

Analysis

The analysis used were basic comparison processes such as counts, means, and tabulations used to identify similarities and differences (Goodrick, 2014) between the cases to create an overview of the offence characteristics.

Results

All the data subjects were male (n = 22), they were given a randomly applied identifying number between 1 and 22, the identifying number bears no significance to their offending.

The perpetrators of all the offences except for those with the identifiers 3 and 4 were convicted of offending independently. The males with identifiers 3 and 4 worked in a "joint-enterprise"'. The reports indicated that 15 people (68.18%) were convicted of online only offending, but within these 4 (18.64%) people's convictions included remote sexual assaults on minors (directing a child to offend against another child). These convictions included the statutory rape of a child under the consenting age by another child victim under the duress and instruction from the person committing the initial offence. Five (22.73%) of the cases included convictions for contact-based sexual offending, and in two (9.09%) cases the defendant had either offered or tried to arrange a physical meeting.

Demographics, Locations, and Sentencing of Those Convicted of Sextortion Offences

The age-at-conviction of the people convicted of sextortion offences (n = 22) ranged from 19 to 42 years old (mean = 30.13 years, mode = 31, median = 31, SD = 6.21).

In 11 (50%) of the cases the person who committed the offence presented as female online, and 14 (63.63%) reported that their age was younger when online. Table 3.1 indicates the locations of the study subjects, with 36.36% in the UK, and 36.36% in the USA.

The data in Table 3.2 present the locations of the person when committing the offence, their victims' locations, and whether offending occurred across an international boundary. Of the total sample 59.1% (n = 13) offended across borders, a much smaller proportion (36.36%) offended within their country of residence. In one case (4.54%), this

Table 3.1 Locations of persons convicted of sextortion offences

Location	*Frequency*
UK	8
USA	8
Australia	3
Netherlands	1
Iraq	1
Romania	1

information was not known. The persons convicted with the identifiers 3 and 4 acted jointly.

Key: O = Online offending only, R = Remote online contact offending, C = Contact offending in person,[2] M = Arranged to meet victim.

Figure 3.1 indicates each defendant's sentencing along with the nation of prosecution and where available the locality. Those who committed contact offences are represented on the graph with unfilled columns. The six longest sentences were passed in cases 2 (110 years) and 3 (105 years) within US courts, for online only offences. The shortest sentence (Case 1, 1.5 years) was passed against an individual who hacked into 100–150 victims' computers from around the world, and subsequently demanded indecent images. Case 16 (UK) involved the remote rape of three children by coercing another child to perform a sexual act, the indictment also included 13 cases of blackmail to obtain indecent images. This person received a lower sentence than some of the online-only cases from within the UK and overseas. Others who committed sexual offences by remotely sexually assaulting child (11,16,17, 22) also received lower sentences than those convicted of online only offences.

Victim Ages

Of the 22 examined cases the victim's sex was male in 4 cases (18.18%), female in 13 cases (59.09%), and both in 5 cases (22.73%). In mixed sex cases, ratios of male to female victims were not reported. A total of 18 (81.81%) of the cases indicated that only children under 18 were

[2] The definition of contact offending used was - "Those who physically commit sexual offences against child victims" (Elliot et al., 2012, p. 4).

Table 3.2 Locations and offending type

Identifier	*Location*	*Victim Location/s*	*Across international boundary*	*Offending type (see key)*
1	California, USA	Canada, Ireland, Moldova, USA	Yes	O
2	Florida, USA	USA, Canada, UK	Yes	O
3	North Carolina, USA	Quoted as "around the world"	Yes	O
4	Baghdad	Quoted as "around the world"	Yes	O
5	Alabama, USA	USA and "internationally"	Yes	O
6	California, USA	USA and "overseas"	Yes	O,C
7	Indiana, USA	USA	No	O
8	Netherlands	Netherlands, Canada	Yes	O
9	Newport UK	UK	No	O, M
10	Melbourne Australia	Australia and "overseas"	Yes	O
11	Melbourne, Australia	Australia, USA, and "overseas"	Yes	O,R
12	California, USA	N/K	N/K	O
13	Oldham, UK	UK	No	O
14	Derbyshire UK	UK, Canada, USA	Yes	O, C
15	Victoria, Australia	Australia	No	O, R
16	Birmingham, UK	UK	No	O, R, C
17	California, USA	USA	No	O, R, C
18	County Durham, UK	UK, USA, Canada, Australia	Yes	O
19	Romania	Northern Ireland	Yes	O
20	Manchester, UK	UK	No	O
21	Staffordshire, UK	UK	No	O, M
22	Birmingham, UK	UK and "worldwide"	Yes	O, R

victimised, with four (18.18%) involving the coercion of both adults and children. From the available data, there were no indications that the victims were previously known to the person convicted of the offence. In 7 (31.82%) of the cases, the victims were reported as being younger than teenagers. The youngest reported victims of blackmail were 8 and 9 years old. However, there were further secondary victims created by the

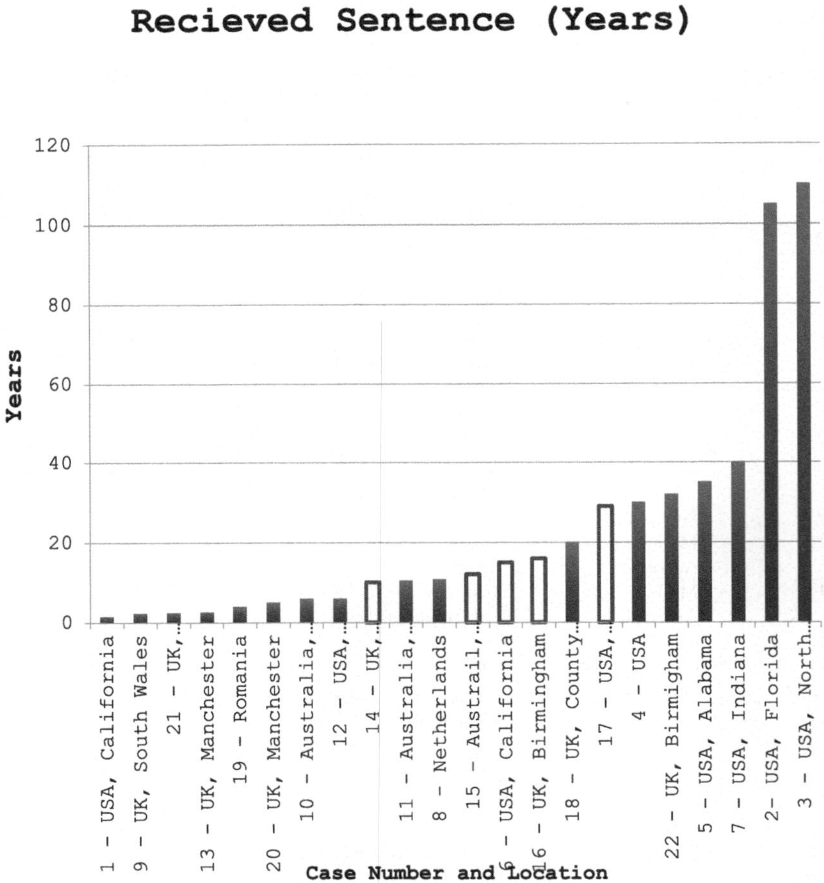

Fig. 3.1 Sentencing duration

coercion of primary victims to perform sex acts against secondary victims (other minors), the youngest being against a 12-month-old baby who was reportedly raped by a blackmail victim under duress (Case 18).

Contact Offending

In 5 (22.73%) of the cases, the defendants had either met with or arranged a meeting with a child victim. In 4 (18.18%) of these cases, it was reported that the person who committed the offence had performed a sex act with a child victim. Three (13.64%) of these were the victims of online coercion/blackmail. In 1 (4.54%) of the cases, police officers found the defendant (case 15) in bed, having just performed sex acts on a child who was not a victim in the initial blackmail investigation. The 15 (68.18%) remaining cases reported no attempted to meet with the victim/s.

Contacting Victim

The most common method used to establish contact with the victims was using social media (17 cases; 77.27%). The remaining cases did not report whether social media was used. Fake or multiple fake profiles would be created on social networking sites. A total of 14 (63.64%) social media alone was used to correspond with their victims. One case did not report the contact method. In the remaining 5 (22.73%) cases, malware was used to access the victim's computers, with chat rooms and social media also being utilised to either communicate with the victim or threaten publication of the information or an account takeover.

Hacking of Victim's Computers

In the 5 (22.73%) cases where hacking or account takeover was identified, all of the cases used some form of Remote Access Trojan (RAT; Europol, 2020). It was disguised in files or attachments the victims were encouraged to download. Once opened they installed a piece of trojan software, (e.g., Bifrostor, Blackshades). These allow the victim's computer to be controlled remotely and covertly by another user, giving the person committing the offence the capability to collect log-in information, mange files and settings, and run processes (Symantec, 2017). Once this level of access to the victim's computer is achieved, they are able to use the computer as their own. In these case studies, defendants were reported to use this access to:

- Identify personal information about the victim or their friends/ family.
- Access computer webcams and (cloud) storage to covertly to obtain images sexual and non-sexual of victims.
- Obtain login information to social media accounts.

- Threaten to destroy files on computer or cause computer to crash/ become unusable.

Coercive Techniques Employed to Procure Images from Victims

In 21 of the 22 cases (95.5%), the person committing the offence threatened to expose an image of the victim on the Internet unless further sexual images were shared. In the majority of cases, this threat was to expose a pre-existing image or piece of information to friends (n = 6, 27.27%), publicly online (n = 5, 22.73%) or on pornography websites (n = 3, 13.64%). Additional tactics were also in seven cases (31.82%). These included threats of revealing victim sexuality (n = 3, 13.64%), physical harm to the victim/their family (n = 1, 4.5%), or reporting the victim to the police for generating/possessing indecent images of children (n = 1, 4.5%). Some of the people convicted also used financial rewards (n = 3, 13.64%) or the restriction/withdrawing of benefits previously given to the victim (n = 1, 4.54%).

Demands

Table 3.3 indicates the style of demands made to the victims. The majority of cases (n = 19, 86.36%) involved demands for indecent imagery—pictures, videos or live streaming, these are summarised in Table 3.4. Some victims were also coerced into personal meetings, physical abuse or abusing other children.

In making demands 22.73% (n = 5) of the cases involved multiple types of requests from victims. In 12 cases (54.46%), the demands made

Table 3.3 Demands made to the victims

Demand	*Frequency*
Nude/sexual pictures	19
Strip/perform sexual acts on camera	7
Money	3
Personal meeting	2
Perform a sexual act against another child	2
Not given	1

Table 3.4 Methods of gaining compromising information

Leverage gained by	*Frequency*
Hacked computer and gained access to webcam obtaining compromising images of victims	3
Hacked computer and obtaining compromising image from stored files	1
Befriended people on social media using fake profile. Sent Malware, hacked computer and threatened to damage it	1
Befriended people on social media using fake profile, developed an online relationship manipulating victim into providing compromising image	15
Befriended people on social media using fake profile, developed an online relationship manipulating victim into providing personal information	1

reportedly became progressively more sexual over time. A small proportion of the cases ($n = 2$, 9.1%) reported financially oriented blackmail against some of the victims for not disclosing their sexuality.

Obtaining Leverage Against a Victim

The online sexual coercion of children relies upon the person's ability to obtain the first victim image or other means of providing leverage to compel a victim to fulfil a demand (Acar, 2016). The most common method used ($n = 17$, 77.27%) was deceiving the victim about their true identity while in a chat room or on a social media platform, and then build an online relationship. In most of these cases ($n = 15$, 68.19%), after establishing this relationship an initial trade of images occurred, providing the necessary material to blackmail the victim. Table 3.4 indicates the frequency of the methods.

Sexual Media and Fake Profiles

As highlighted fake online profile use was common. Of those using social media or chat rooms, 14 (63.64%) presented themselves as someone younger, 12 (54.5%) posed as a female, 6 (27.27%) presented as male, and 3 (13.64%) posed as both male and female. Further, two people (9.10%) posed as Justin Bieber while committing the offence, and one (4.54%) as a modelling agent. Table 3.5 indicates the frequency an individual social media sites was named as being used in coercing sexual images from children.

Table 3.5 Frequency of social media site usage

Facebook	*11*
Myspace	2
Omegle	2
Stickam	1
Meetme	1
Habbo	1
Kik	1
Whatsapp	1
BBM	1
Snapchat	1

Number of Victims

Table 3.6 provides the number of victims from each case. While the number of victims were not a case selection criterion, it is noted that typically larger cases garner more police and media attention. In cases where no victim numbers were reported, a minimum of one was given (even if numerous charges were made). The proved victim numbers are the minimum number of victims available and those used in court proceedings. The suspected victim numbers are the number of victims that are believed to have been targeted as described in the reporting of the cases. Where it was not possible to establish this number, the actual number of victims from the charges was used. In all cases, the minimum number from the estimates has been used. For example, in case 13, communication with the case officer revealed that 21 child victims were identified, but the prosecution relied on evidence from one victim.

The number of victims in both categories (proved and suspected) is high. The proved victim number totals 456 victims among 22 defendants (mean = 20.72, median = 9.5). The suspected victim number multiplies this by a factor of ~ 12 to a total of 5505 victims between the 22 defendants (mean = 250.23, median = 24).

Offending Period

Table 3.7 presents the identifiable, reported period over which the people committed the offences. There does not appear to be any correlation between the length of offending time and the number of victims or sentence duration. For example, the two longest offending periods (Cases 15 [Australia] and 22 [UK]) both included remote sexual assaults/offending against victims but did not receive proportionally

Table 3.6 Number of victims per defendant

Case Identifier	*Proved victim numbers*	*Suspected victim numbers*	*Sentence*
1	12	100	18 months
2	1	350	105 years
3	1	3800	110 years
4	-	-	30 years
5	15	15	35 years
6	12	24	15 years
7	20	153	40 years
8	20	250	10 years 243 days
9	3	3	28 months
10	17	17	6 years
11	43	43	10 years 5 months
12	230	230	72 months
13	1	21	32 months
14	4	4	10 years
15	22	22	12 years
16	1	63	16 years
17	1	1	29 years
18	19	100	20 years
19	1	1	4 years
20	7	7	Indeterminate sentence—minimum of 5 years
21	1	1	2 1/2 years
22	45	300	32 years
Total	456	5505	

long sentences, instead ranking 11th and 5th on the sentencing chart (Fig. 3.1). The shortest offending periods (Cases 13 [UK] and 19 [Romania]) ranked 19th and 18th on the sentencing chart. The different legal systems included in the sample tended to show that those convicted within the US jurisdiction on average got longer sentences than other countries (see Fig. 3.1).

The mean sentence in the USA was 40.28 years opposed to the UK for example, which was 12.17 years, the sample size was not sufficient to provide an accurate representation for examples from other countries.

Table 3.7 Period of offending

Case identifier	*From*	*To*	*Period of offending (years)*	*Legal jurisdiction*
13	2007	2007	< 1	UK
19	June-15	June-15	< 1	Romania
21	2015	2015	< 1	UK
1	2012	2013	1	UK
6	2012	2013	1	USA
12	2009	2010	1	USA
5	2009	2011	2	USA
7	2010	2012	2	USA
11	2011	2013	2	USA
14	2003	2005	2	Australia
17	2011	2013	2	UK
2	2007	2010	3	USA
9	2012	2015	3	USA
10	2009	2012	3	UK
20	2008	2011	3	Australia
3	2005	2009	4	UK
4	2005	2009	4	USA
16	2011	2016	5	USA
8	2008	2014	6	UK
22	2009	2017	8	Netherland
15	2006	2015	9	UK
18	–	–	–	Australia

Detection Avoidance

Detection avoidance methods used by people who were convicted varied in sophistication. In 2 (9.09%) of the cases involving hacking took steps to hide their Internet Protocol (IP) addresses, using either virtual IP addresses or IP cloaking, making identification more difficult. In the remaining hacking (3) cases, no steps were taken to hide IP addresses, but false names were used on social media/email accounts. One of these, one used his workplace IP address while committing the offence. Of the 17 non-hacking cases, only two people used tactics to hide an IP address while committing the offences. It may be worth noting that even when steps were taken to avoid detection, the authorities were still able to trace the person who was committing the offence using a variety of conventional or covert investigative methods. Some of which included simply checking registration with Internet service providers, account registration details, or cross-checking multiple identities for common data. Only one of the cases involved more sophisticated methods (data encryption) to avoid detection.

Discussion

There were some common themes found within the studied offending style. Online sexual coercion of children on the Internet appeared to be a form of criminality predominantly committed by males, with those responsible targeting numerous victims over a prolonged period of time. The criminality does not seem to be limited to online-only offending, with just under a quarter of the cases involving contact offending. Further, some of the people convicted were found to have coerced the initial child victims to commit sexual offences against their siblings or friends. One highlighted case included the rape of a 12-month-old baby by a victim (in the USA) who was under duress from a person in the UK.

This criminality falls within the remit of cybercrime (Burden & Palmer, 2003): crimes enabled by the Internet, potentially across international boundaries. This introduces jurisdictional difficulties in the form of ownership, information disclosure and legal process. It makes the detection and prosecution of the defendant slower and more difficult, but not insurmountable. Protocols are in place (CPS, 2013; NPIA, 2012) to assist this. This study has shown that cross-border enforcement protocols are needed, along with the specialist knowledge to apply them. Their application requires more time and inter-jurisdiction cooperations compared to domestic investigations. Because of this, cases of online sexual coercion are likely to benefit from being allocated to specialist investigative departments with the knowledge and capacity to perform this. This will further the ability to establish the extent of victimisation and allow sentencing to reflect this.

Although sentencing tended to attract a substantial custodial period for those who progressed to contact offences, the largest sentences were for non-contact offences committed in the USA. Given that over 50% of the cases involved transnational communications, a joint, consistent international sentencing policy is worthy of consideration as a deterrent to counter cross-border sextortion. This supports the recommendations of previous research (e.g., Wittes et al., 2016).

In the majority of the cases, victims provided self-generated sexual images or video to a person who they believed was someone else. The person committing the sextortion subsequently used this as leverage to coerce the victim into providing further imagery. Targeted prevention advice about the creation, storage and production of explicit images might reduce the images available to be used as leverage. But this is already in place for most children going through the education systems in the countries subject to this study. This suggests a stronger preventative method is needed such as the filtering of images suspected to contain sexual content or moderation of sexually suggestive conversations among those below the age of consent. These processes could be automated and/or performed manually.

The number of people using sophisticated methods to avoid detection while committing offences was low. Most used fake details for registering online accounts. Being able to create multiple fake social media accounts on platforms such as Facebook means the barriers to entry for this crime type are low (The person from case 18 had over 30 accounts). Making multiple/fake accounts could be made more difficult. Safeguarding guidance provides an obligation to discharge duties in promoting child welfare. This includes controlling how those considered high risk to the welfare of children are allowed access (HM Government, 2018). Extending these obligations to industries and platforms that allow open communication and easy access to children may require some consideration, especially when it is known such abuse has resulted in suicides. From the cases studied it is worth noting that even those who tried to hide their IP address and identity were brought to justice. Once a notification was made to the authorities, they were able to trace and detect the people who had committed the offence using a variety of means. These included checking registrations with service providers, or cross-checking of multiple identities for common registration information. While there may be a perception of anonymity on the Internet, identification by the authorities is a realistic prospect. It is achieved through conventional investigative methods. But without a report or notification only those crimes proactively investigated will ever be detected. For someone to commit 3800 offences (Cases 3 and 4) or have 27 hard drives full of 20,400 images (Case 8), there is clearly a problem with the notification of online offending. The case studies provide only an initial glimpse into online sexual coercion, it seems that those committing these offences become involved in a protracted period of repeat offending against children. Within this study, 27.27% ($n = 6$) of the cases included offending periods of over 4 years, and 81.82% ($n = 18$) of them offended for a period in excess of a year.

The majority of threats were to expose compromising pictures of the victims to peers and family. The impact of the threat was sufficient to force the victims to comply and provide further indecent images, causing trauma for the victims, and in some cases potentially contributing to a death by suicide. This is a reminder that online sexual coercion should not be underestimated (Kopecký, 2017). Providing a route for victims of sextortion to follow should be paramount to protect victims and help them seek support. As the organisations who do this already exist, sign-posting and awareness may need improvement. Algorithmic social media programmes could be used to try and push information to children (and adults) who may be vulnerable.

Within the case studies, a variety of offences comprised the prosecutions, including blackmail, rape, enticement, solicitation and computer misuse. There were no reports of insufficient statute to pursue prosecution. Wittes et al. (2016) highlight the lack of an offence of sextortion. While the lack of a specific offence entitled sextortion is problematised (Wittes et al., 2016), it is not clear if (and assessing the prevalence of the issue) this would improve prosecution rates. In the UK, guidance exists outlining how online sexual crimes should be categorised and processed (College of policing, 2016; CPS, 2013). It seems that the processes and law are in place to put authorities into an informed position to tackle crimes of this type. But the high number of victims suggests that interventions may need improvement or accelerated implementation. Though it is noted that attitudinal barriers to reporting may also exist, as victims may feel unable to report due to shame, self-blame, or threats made by the person who is blackmailing them. Similarly, responses to reports should be positive and supportive, and victims should be signposted to emotional/social support if necessary.

The concept of remote sexual offending is introduced when examining these cases. The person committing the offence directs sexual activities of primary victims, making them commit sexual offences and creating secondary victims who are potentially abused in far more serious ways. Briggs et al.'s (2011) study of internet chat room offending explained how there were two types of Internet-based offending, cases where the individual had a desire to engage in offline sexual practices, and those who were interested in cybersex. With the online category showing less severe criminogenic factors than other categories. The remote sexual offending cases do not seem to adhere to this hypothesis, with some of the most serious sexual offences being committed by people who offended exclusively online.

Limitations

This study collected data from a variety of sources in an unstandardised format and made generalisations from it to understand the subject matter. It has not been produced under scientific conditions and cannot claim to provide a statistical guidance. Future research into this subject area should more rigorous methods to detect patterns or trends highlighted within this chapter. The case study searches were conducted in 2017. Search engine results and website content changes with time. The results returned in 2017 may not be achievable in later years. Similar searches conducted might report on different cases and aspects of criminality which would change the key data found within the reports used in this study. While comment is made of the range of sentences passed in different legal jurisdictions, it is also recognised that sentencing and legal powers are different within these jurisdictions. To fully explore whether sentencing is consistent fully representative samples within the various jurisdictions would be required.

This study took an initial look into the incidence of sextortion, how it happens, who commits it and how they do it. It revealed that sextortion crimes are committed across international boundaries, victimise many children, and continue offending until they are caught. It provides the foundations for understanding how online sexual coercion develops and begins to comment on potential implications for Internet safety and legal processes and regulations that could be implemented to reduce perpetration and victimisation of sextortion offences.

References

Acar, K. V. (2016). Sexual extortion of children in cyberspace. *International Journal of Cyber Criminology, 10*(2), 110–126. https://doi.org/10.5281/zenodo.163398/

Altman, S. (1993). A patchwork theory of blackmail. *University of Pennsylvania Law Review, 141*(5), 1639–1661. https://doi.org/10.2307/3312570

Black, P. J., Wollis, M., Woodworth, M., & Hancock, J. T. (2015). A linguistic analysis of grooming strategies of online child sex offenders: Implications for our understanding of predatory sexual behavior in an increasingly computer-mediated world. *Child Abuse & Neglect, 44*(140–149), 1. https://doi.org/10.1016/j.chiabu.2014.12.004

Briggs, P., Simon, W. T., & Simonsen, S. (2011). An exploratory study of internet-initiated sexual offenses and the chat room sex offender: Has the internet enabled a new typology of sex offender? *Sexual Abuse, 23*(1), 72–91. https://doi.org/10.1177/1079063210384275

Burden, K., & Palmer, C. (2003). Internet crime: Cyber crime—a new breed of criminal? *Computer Law & Security Report, 19*(3), 222–227. https://doi.org/10.1016/S0267-3649(03)00306-6

Child Exploitation and Online Protection Centre. (2010). Child exploitation and online protection centre: The way forward [Accessed: 23/09/2024] https://assets.publishing.service.gov.uk/media/5a7c1a9140f0b61a825d6797/7785.pdf

College of policing. (2016). Police action in response to youth produced sexual imagery ('Sexting'). https://library.college.police.uk/docs/college-of-policing/briefing-note-sexting-2016.pdf

Conte, J. R., Wolf, S., & Smith, T. (1989). What sexual offenders tell us about prevention strategies. *Child Abuse & Neglect, 13*(2), 293–301. https://doi.org/10.1016/0145-2134(89)90016-1

Crown Prosecution Service. (2013). *Child sexual abuse: Guidelines on prosecuting cases of child sexual abuse.* https://www.cps.gov.uk/legal-guidance/child-sexual-abuse-guidelines-prosecuting-cases-child-sexual-abuse

Crown Prosecution Service. (2023). *Child sexual abuse: Guidelines on prosecuting cases of child sexual abuse.* [Accessed: 23/09/2024] https://www.cps.gov.uk/legal-guidance/child-sexual-abuse-guidelines-prosecuting-cases-child-sexual-abuse

DeFrancis, V. (1969). *Protecting the child victim of sex crimes committed by adults.* American Humane Association Children's Division.

Dehue, F., Bolman, C., & Völlink, T. (2008). Cyberbullying: Youngsters' experiences and parental perception. *Cyberpsychology & Behavior, 11*(2), 217–223. https://doi.org/10.1089/cpb.2007.0008

Elliott, I. A., Beech, A. R., & Mandeville-Norden, R. (2012). The psychological profiles of internet, contact, and mixed internet/contact sex offenders. *Sexual Abuse, 25*(1), 3–20. https://doi.org/10.1177/1079063212439426

Europol European Cybercrime Centre (2015). *Virtual global taskforce: Child sexual exploitation environmental scan 2015.* [Accessed: 23/09/2024] https://www.europol.europa.eu/media-press/newsroom/news/2015-vgt-child-sexual-exploitation-environmental-scan

Federal Bureau of Investigation. (2016). *Sextortion affecting thousands of U.S. children.* [Accessed: 23/09/2024] https://www.fbi.gov/contact-us/field-offices/charlotte/news/press-releases/sextortion-affecting-thousands-of-u-s-children

Finkelhor, D., Mitchell, K. J., & Wolak, J. (2000). *Online victimization: A report on the nation's youth.* Department of Justice. https://www.ojp.gov/pdffiles1/Digitization/188393NCJRS.pdf

Forward, S., & Frazier, D. (1996). *Emotional blackmail.* Quill.

Goertz, G., & Levy, J. S. (2007). Causal explanation, necessary conditions, and case studies. In J. Levy & G. Goertz (Eds.), *Explaining War and Peace* (pp. 25–62). Routledge.

Goodrick, D. (2014). Comparative case studies. [Accessed: 23/09/2024] http://www.dmeforpeace.org/wp-content/uploads/2017/06/Comparative_Case_Studies_ENG.pdf

Henry, N., Flynn, A., & Powell, A. (2018). Policing image-based sexual abuse: Stakeholder perspectives. *Police Practice & Research, 19*(6), 565–581. https://doi.org/10.1080/15614263.2018.1507892

Her Majesties Inspectorate of Constabularies. (2016). Improving policing across Scotland crime audit 2016. [Accessed: 23/09/2024] http://www.hmics.org/sites/default/files/publications/HMICS%20Crime%20Audit%202016.pdf

Kopecký, K. (2017). Online blackmail of Czech children focused on so-called "sextortion" (analysis of culprit and victim behaviors). *Telematics and Informatics, 34*(1), 11–19. https://doi.org/10.1016/j.tele.2016.04.004

Kopecký, K., René, S., & Veronika, K. (2014). *Risks of internet communication IV. centre for prevention of risky virtual communication.* Olomouc, Czech Republic. [Accessed: 23/09/2024] https://www.researchgate.net/publication/259558616_Risks_of_internet_communication_IV_-_research_report

Krone, T. (2004). *A typology of online child pornography offending (279; Trends and issues in crime and criminal justice).* Australian Institute of Criminology. https://www.researchgate.net/publication/237371926_A_Typology_of_Online_Child_Pornography_Offending

Lang, R. A., & Frenzel, R. R. (1988). How sex offenders lure children. *Annals of Sex Research, 1*(2), 303–317. https://doi.org/10.1177/107906328800100207

National Policing Improvement Agency, (NPIA). (2012). *European cross-border investigations 2012 Association of chief police officers*. [Accessed: 23/09/2024] http://library.college.police.uk/docs/appref/european-cross-border-investigations.pdf

O'Malley, R. L., & Holt, K. M. (2020). Cyber sextortion: An exploratory analysis of different perpetrators engaging in a similar crime. *Journal of Interpersonal Violence, 37*(1–2), 258–283. https://doi.org/10.1177/0886260520909186

Patchin, J. W., & Hinduja, S. (2018). Sextortion among adolescents: Results from a national survey of U.S. youth. *Sexual Abuse, 32*(1), 30–54. https://doi.org/10.1177/1079063218800469

Peelo, M., & Soothill, K. (2014). 'Marginal' crime: The example of blackmail in representing evolving crime narratives. *The Howard Journal of Criminal Justice, 53*(3), 221–236. https://doi.org/10.1111/hojo.12061

Raven, B. H. (2008). The bases of power and the power/interaction model of interpersonal influence. *Analyses of Social Issues and Public Policy, 8*(1), 1–22. https://doi.org/10.1111/j.1530-2415.2008.00159.x

Robinson, P. H., Cahill, M. T., & Bartels, D. M. (2010). Competing theories of blackmail: An empirical research critique of criminal law theory. *Texas Law Review, 89*(2), 291. https://www.proquest.com/scholarly-journals/competing-theories-blackmail-empirical-research/docview/866633048/se-2?accountid=14693

Rosenthal, R., & Rosnow, R. L. (2009). *Artifacts in behavioral research*. Oxford University Press.

Staksrud, E., Ólafsson, K., & Livingstone, S. (2013). Does the use of social networking sites increase children's risk of harm? *Computers in Human Behavior, 29*(1), 40–50. https://doi.org/10.1016/j.chb.2012.05.026

Taylor, M., & Qualye, E. (2006). The internet and abuse images of children: Search, precriminal situations and opportunity. In R. Wortley & S. Smallbone (Eds.) *Situational prevention of child sexual abuse. Crime prevention studies* (pp.169–195). Criminal Justice Press & Willow Tree Press, USA.

US Department of Justice. (2016). The national strategy for child exploitation prevention and interdiction—Report to congress. [Accessed: 23/09/2024] https://www.justice.gov/psc/national-strategy-child-exploitation-prevention-and-interdiction

Webster, S., Davidson, J., Bifulco, A., Gottschalk, P., Carettir, V., & Tompkins, C. (2012). European online grooming project. [Accessed: 23/09/2024] http://natcen.ac.uk/media/22514/european-online-grooming-projectfinalreport.pdf

Wittes, B., Poplin C., Jurecic Q., & Spera C. (2016). Sextortion: Cybersecurity, teenagers, and remote sexual assault. [Accessed: 23/09/2024] https://www.brookings.edu/research/sextortion-cybersecurity-teenagers-and-remote-sexual-assault/

Wolak, J., & Finkelhor, D. (2016). Sextortion: Findings from a survey of 1631 victims. Durham, NH: Crimes against children research center. [Accessed: 23/09/2024] http://www.unh.edu/ccrc/pdf/Sextortion_RPT_FNL_rev0803.pdf

Wright, J., & Javid, S. (2020). Online harms white paper [Government]. gov.uk. [Accessed: 23/09/2024] https://www.gov.uk/government/consultations/online-harms-white-paper/online-harms-white-paper

Yin, R. K. (2018). *Case study research and applications* (Sixth ed.). Sage.

CHAPTER 4

Image-Based Sexual Abuse

Dean Fido and Craig A. Harper

Defining Image-Based Sexual Abuse

The term *image-based sexual abuse* (IBSA) envelopes a range of behaviours involving the non-consensual generation, taking, and/or distribution of private sexual images, where *'images'* refers to both physical and digital media. Though previously discussed comprehensively in socio-legal spheres (Henry et al., 2017; McGlynn et al., 2017), more recent publications have sought to frame the understanding of this phenomenon from the perspective of forensic psychology (see Fido et al., 2021, 2022; Fido & Harper, 2020). Harper et al. (2021)

D. Fido (✉)
University of Derby, Derby, UK
e-mail: d.fido@derby.ac.uk

C. A. Harper
Nottingham Trent University, Nottingham, UK
e-mail: craig.harper@ntu.ac.uk

C. A. Harper et al. (eds.), *Sexual Crime and the Internet*, Sexual Crime,
https://doi.org/10.1007/978-3-031-95844-1_4

describe a taxonomic framework of image-based sexual abuse that separates out behaviours including *revenge pornography*[1], *upskirting*, *deepfake media production*, and *cyber-flashing*; framing each as being conceptually distinct, and each as important to understand as the next. In the sections below, we briefly describe and provide context for each of these behaviours.

Revenge Pornography

Revenge pornography describes the non-consensual distribution of private, explicit images of another without their consent and with the intention to cause harm (e.g., through embarrassment and/or distress). Though by no means always the cause, revenge pornography (or threat thereof) commonly results from the breakdown of a relationship (Dawkins, 2015; Hall & Hearn, 2018) and serves as a means of coercing, shaming, or in other ways damaging the reputation of the other party (Henry & Powell, 2014). The modern history of revenge pornography and its associated discourse typically refers to dedicated websites such as IsAnyoneUp.com, whereby sexual images were uploaded with accompanying private information including telephone numbers, work addresses, and social media accounts (Visser, 2012). In popular media, this phenomenon has even been the subject of the 2022 three-part Netflix docuseries '*The Most Hated Man on the Internet*', wherein the story of this website, and its creator, Hunter Moore, is told. However, as revenge pornography is now criminalised across much of the world, this overt and identifiable approach is no longer a viable means of offending behaviour; with such offences now typically committed in less overt and extravagant ways, such as sharing images within WhatsApp and Telegram groups (Harper et al., 2021).

Victims of revenge pornography consistently face social (e.g., embarrassment, hampered reputation), financial (e.g., loss of employment), and health (e.g., depression, anxiety, stress) consequences. With the existence of cases resulting in self-harm and suicide completion (Stroud, 2014),

[1] The authors recognise the negative discourse around the term 'revenge porn(ography)', in that it both places blame on the victim through the term revenge and also suggests that the acts depicted are always consensual through the term pornography (see Fido & Harper, 2020). However, this term has been used here as this is the more common and lay-term for such act.

the impact of this behaviour should not be discarded. Moreover, the impact of revenge pornography is not just immediate and short lived. Once such images have been shared online, they can be downloaded and redistributed, even when the original image has been removed (Lichter, 2013). As such, victims are likely to experience re-victimisation, which can occur unexpectedly at key points within their lives. Critics of victims of revenge pornography within the general public have previously attributed their victimisation to 'reckless', 'careless', and 'naive' behaviour of sharing such images in the first place (Henry & Powell, 2015a), but it is important to remember the role that sharing sexual images plays in forming and maintaining sexual relationships in the modern day. It is equally important to note that even if consent is provided in the first instance (the initial sharing), this consent does not extend to subsequent sharing (Henry & Powell, 2016).

Relative to the other types of IBSA discussed throughout this chapter, revenge pornography is the most explored behaviour across legal, criminological, and forensic spheres. Hall and Hearn (2019) suggest that revenge pornography might be selected as a response option as a means of evidencing the perpetrator's sexual prowess and their ability to gain attractive mates, such as through boasting about one's sexual conquests. Other avenues of investigation might frame revenge pornography as an atypical coping strategy to the breakdown of a relationship (Field et al., 2009) whereby the perpetrator seeks to combat negative affective states (e.g., anger, anxiety, or loneliness). This is a compelling argument that mirrors findings contextualised in physical sexual behaviours (Walton et al., 2017). It is thought that being in such negative states might lead to the suppression of empathic responses to the victims of one's crimes (Howells et al., 2004) and as such, ultimately result in poor behavioural control and reduced ability to inhibit one's deviant behaviour (Quayle & Taylor, 2002). Such positions have been framed as motivators in deviant sexual and online behaviours elsewhere (Jonason & Kavanagh, 2010; Wright et al., 2019).

Upskirting

'Upskirting' is a colloquial term that describes the non-consensual and surreptitious capturing of intimate images under a non-consenting (or even aware) individual's clothing, with the intention of viewing their genitals or buttocks to obtain sexual gratification, or to cause humiliation, distress, or alarm (Ministry of Justice, 2019). This offence is typically perpetrated by individuals who hold atypical sexual interests (McManus et al., 2013), who may be motivated by a perceived entitlement to sex (Pemberton & Wakeling, 2009) and power imbalance over others (Beech & Mann, 2002). Hall et al. (2022) recent discussion of comments made on The Candid Forum; a website dedicated to sharing images of women in public, highlighted an array of perceptions that although included misogynistic attitudes, also highlighted expressions of appreciation of the depicted women's bodies and beauty, as well as comments pertaining to the 'skill' of the male photographer.

Upskirting could be classified as a paraphilia related to voyeurism, potentially manifesting as a result of an abnormality in the perpetrator's sexual interest (McManus et al., 2013). Aligning upskirting with voyeurism, extant literature suggests that such perpetrators might have overall lower levels of sexual satisfaction, engage in substance abuse, suffer from poor interpersonal relationships, and be pre-disposed to becoming at risk for poor mental well-being (Långström & Seto, 2006). In such cases, upskirting would act as a conduit to obtaining a level of sexual satisfaction that they cannot achieve in tandem with another person. It might also be the case that upskirting is associated with a perceived entitlement to sex (Pemberton & Wakeling, 2009)—an implicit theory also associated with rape and child molestation (Beech & Mann, 2002)—wherein those who engage in upskirting capture non-consensual images of another as a means of taking what they want.

In consideration of broader personality traits that might play a role in the consumption of upskirting or the proclivity to engage in upskirting, the personality trait of psychopathy might play an active role.[2] For example, psychopathy has previously been shown to moderate the effects of pornography consumption on sexual behaviour (Williams et al., 2009), with psychopathy, narcissism, and Machiavellianism together predicting sensation seeking, a desire for sexual stimulation, and behaviours related to seizing opportunities to achieve sexual gratification (Jonason et al., 2012). Of direct relevance to upskirting, Fido et al. (2023) recently evidenced a direct relationship between increased self-reported psychopathic personality traits and proclivity to engage in upskirting behaviour.

[2] In this instance, we are referring to higher degrees of psychopathic personality traits that exist to some degree in everyone within the general population, and not a clinical presence of psychopathy.

In practice, this suggests a need to further explore, delineate, and contextualise predictors of upskirting and the propensity to seek out and impulsively obtain sexual gratification.

Deepfake Media Production

Deepfake media production refers to the superimposition (via machine learning software) of the likeness of an individual onto the body of another (Rofer, 2016). Though this technique has the potential to generate harmless (or even humorous) media, it is more commonly used as a means of producing sexualised images of a target individual (Hickey, 2018). This is referred to as 'deepfake' porn. Typically, deepfake videos target female celebrities (e.g., Jennifer Lawrence, Emma Watson); victimising them through the superimposition of their faces onto the bodies of pornography actresses (Delfino, 2019). Save for a small handful of studies, there is very little empirical psychological research conducted that focuses on predictors to engage in deepfake media production. Despite the sudden and pervasive growth of the use of deepfake media production, one such study, Fido et al. (2022) demonstrated that on average, only around 5% of the general population within their studies had pre-existing knowledge of deepfaking. This suggests a need for more education and understanding about deepfake media production.

What makes deepfake media production so impactful is that the software required to engage in such behaviour is freely available and easy-to-use—thus enabling anyone to engage in this type of IBSA. More broadly, media generated in this manner can be used to blackmail and extort money from those depicted within them, who seek to halt the release of compromising images of themselves regardless of whether they are real or not. From a psychological and cognitive perspective, viewing sexually explicit material plays a role in the generation and maintenance of sexual cognitive scripts that help to shape our understanding of normative, appropriate, and rewarding sexual behaviour (Wright et al., 2019). Malformation and deviations in such scripts have been associated with a range of sexual offending (Ward & Beech, 2006; 2016; Ward & Siegert, 2002), and in the IBSA sphere may lead to the generation and dissemination of deepfake pornography as a means of fulfilling sexual curiosity and achieving sexual satisfaction. Nevertheless, it is also important to recognise and acknowledge wider societal reasons as to why somebody might engage in deepfake media production. As highlighted in a Japanese report that documented one of the first arrests for deepfaking (Japan Gazette, October 2, 2020), one of the core motivations provided by the perpetrators for engaging in such behaviour was for the financial gain. Indeed, there is a growing market for such imagery and as such it would be useful for future research to tease apart the unique interactions between psychological and societal motivators.

Cyber-Flashing

Cyber-flashing refers to the unsolicited sharing of sexually explicit images via digital technologies to unsuspecting and non-consenting recipients. Such technologies might include text messaging and social media messaging, and in some higher profile instances, the use of Bluetooth r Apple's AirDrop facilities. Colloquially, and despite it being possible for this type of behaviour to be carried out by females, readers may be more familiar with terms such as 'dick pics', which describe the act of men sending images of their penis to another (Waling & Pym, 2019). Around 50% of college students (Drouin & Landgraff, 2012) and 41% of women aged between 18 and 36 years (Thompson, 2019) report having been sent sexually explicit images or videos, with such high prevalence indicating an imperative need to safeguard such recipients from potential distress. It is also important to be mindful that cyber-flashing specifically refers to unsolicited images, which have the potential to target anybody, and not solicited sexual images which are frequently sent and received during the formation and maintenance of intimate relationships. That being said, there is discussion needed as to the potential role (from the perspective of the perpetrator) that cyber-flashing plays in the facilitating of short-term mating and sexual hook-ups (Fido & Harper, 2020) and how such behaviour might be 'normalised' by the context of fast-paced online dating apps which place a large emphasis on the visual representation (Garcia et al., 2012).

Cyber-flashing encompasses behaviour that is both non-consensual and intrusive to the receiver. As such, there are indeed links between cyber-flashing and exhibitionism, whereby individuals (most notably men; Långström & Seto, 2016) expose themselves to others for sexual pleasure. In line with the psychological literature pertaining to exhibitionism, these perpetrators are likely to score higher on indices of sexual sensation-seeking, substance misuse, and poor psychological adjustment (Långström & Seto, 2006). Moreover, these individuals are likely to have had a high number of sexual partners and have engaged in deviant sexual fantasies about others (Långström & Seto, 2006). Further drawing upon the exhibitionistic literature, perpetrators are likely to be younger men (Långström & Seto, 2006) who present higher levels of dark triad traits (psychopathy, narcissism, and Machiavellianism; Jonason et al., 2009); traits which coincidentally predict greater levels of engagement in short-term mating strategies and a propensity to engage in sexual relationships with the absence of commitment (see Figueredo et al., 2013). As such, despite a lack of cyber-flashing specific literature, the literature which can be drawn upon from a wider array of arenas indicates a key role of sexual arousal and entitlement in cyber-flashing. This would incidentally map onto broader models of sexual offending, such as Seto's (2019) motivation-facilitation model, as well as theories of deviant sexual scripts and cognitions highlighted elsewhere (Ward & Siegert, 2002).

Judgements and Social Beliefs

The second part of this chapter focuses on the extant research on social judgements and beliefs pertaining to IBSA. Moreover, we will comment on how such relationships might be further moderated by victim and perpetrator characteristics, legality, and perceived culpability.

Drawing from the broader physical sexual abuse literature, it is important to contextualise the following discussion within the existence of myths pertinent to sexual abuse. Described *rape mythology*, such myths represent a complex set of prejudicial, stereotyped, and false beliefs about rape victims, rape perpetrators, and the crime of rape itself (Burt, 1980). Together, they place blame on the victim and provide a set of excuses for the actions of the perpetrator of their crimes. The endorsement of such stereotypical beliefs is likely also to affect attitudes towards revenge pornography and its victims as has been evidenced in Henry and Powell (2015b) where victims of revenge pornography were perceived as reckless', 'careless', and 'naive' due to them sharing their private sexual images in the first place. As such, there is a distinct need to not only understand whether such beliefs are equally prevalent in the arena of IBSA but also how—if at all—they differ, as well as personality traits which might best predict their manifestation.

Recently, Harper et al. (2022) published and validated the Beliefs about Revenge Pornography Questionnaire (BRPQ). Items for the BRPQ were developed following a thorough review of the extant literature pertaining to the characteristics of perpetrators of revenge pornography and their victims, indices of judgements, and existing questionnaires that measure rape myths and beliefs about sexual offending in a broader sense. Following statistical analysis (and after removing superfluous factors which did not meet rigid statistical standards), four key factors were identified. Factor one was labelled 'Victims as Promiscuous' (15 items; $\alpha = 0.94$) and related to themes around the characteristics of victims' sexuality and sexual behaviour that might make them more vulnerable to becoming victims of IBSA. Factor two was labelled 'Victim Harm' (13 items; $\alpha = 0.87$) and represents items that link to the deleterious effects of being a victim of revenge pornography and the need for support and protection. Factor three was labelled 'Avoiding Vulnerable Behavior' (10 items; $\alpha = 0.90$) and reflected the strategies people might use to avoid becoming a victim of revenge pornography. Factor four was labelled 'Offense Minimization' (7 items; $\alpha = 0.74$) and reflects the downplaying of the effects of revenge pornography.

Consistent with expectations, those with higher levels of empathy were less likely to blame victims of revenge pornography, with victim blame positively associated with political conservatism. Moreover, believing that the world is just and fair, dark personality traits (e.g., psychopathy, narcissism, and sadism), and higher levels of rape myth acceptance (to evidence how perceptions of IBSA might align with those pertaining to physical sexual abuse) were all also associated with a greater propensity to place blame on the victims of revenge pornography. Such relationships reversed when examining constructs associated with seeing revenge pornography as a sexual offence.

Within Harper et al. (2022), the BRPQ was also used as a means of predicting one's proclivity to engage in revenge pornography wherein proclivity was found to be significantly associated with lower levels of empathy, higher levels of belief in a just world and dark triad personality traits, and the belief that victims of revenge pornography offending are in some way responsible for their experiences. In practice, results of this nature indicate that the BRPQ provides the premier means of understanding one's perceptions and beliefs about victims and perpetrators of revenge pornography whilst simultaneously starting to elicit some of the potential cognitive distortions pertaining to this offence.

Traits Associated with Lenient Judgements

Throughout Hall and Hearn (2018), some perpetrators highlighted that their motivations to perpetrate revenge pornography were a form of boasting about their own sexual exploits in addition to seeking revenge for the perceived actions of their victims. Such boasting aligns well with the notion of *intrasexual competition*; an evolutionary concept defined by the competition between oneself and a sexual rival in the pursuit or retention of sexual and romantic partners (Arnocky & Vaillancourt, 2017). In practice, this might manifest in the form of individuals competing with one another through the accumulation of status such as high-powered or well-paying jobs (Griskevicius et al., 2007) or physical appearance (Dubbs et al., 2017). Here, the use of intrasexual competition would manifest as a means of downplaying their rivals' worth.

In the context of IBSA, specifically engagement in the distribution of non-consensual sexual images of another, there are clear implications for intrasexual competition. Across two samples, Fido et al. (2019) reported positive associations between intrasexual competition and more lenient judgements of revenge pornography. That is, higher levels of intrasexual competition related to more accepting attitudes towards those who committed revenge pornography; a finding which has implications for discourse related to public perceptions. Of interest, when teasing these results apart by participant sex (used as a moderator variable) there was an unexpected trend such that *higher* levels of intrasexual competition were associated with *more lenient* judgements of revenge pornography when the perpetrator was also a female. One potential explanation for this finding relates to possible heightened rates of intrasexual competition being observed among women and their association with increased rates of sexual selfie-taking (Blake et al., 2018). This would suggest that such women may attempt to sexualise themselves as a means of competing with their rivals (possibly as a way of attracting more male sexual partners) and as such the findings of Fido et al. (2019) might reflect such women affirming the experiences of women who have shared sexualised images, rather than marginalising them.

Victim Blaming vs. Situational Crime Prevention

Despite our concerns earlier in this chapter about the potential for victims of revenge pornography to be blamed for their victimisation, data from the USA suggest overwhelming support for the criminalization of the non-consensual sharing of sexual images—particularly among female respondents. However, as predicted, and perhaps worryingly, such support is diminished in situations whereby victims initially produced the images themselves. This finding therefore mirrors reports of women who have higher rates of provocative selfie-taking being implicated in higher degrees of victim blaming (Mann & Smith, 2020). As such, with the victim often being the one to initially send such images (Hall & Hearn, 2018), victim blaming will likely play a key role in judgements of the harm caused by revenge pornography offending.

Seemingly, victim blaming in the context of cases featuring IBSA stems from the role that victims are perceived to take during the initial taking and dissemination of private sexual images. Though apathy is generally provided to such victims (Fay, 2018), a broader understanding of potential moderators of this would act as a useful tool for not only offering support for victims but for informing legal processes and media representations pertaining to this group. To date, there is no research associated with this line of theory, but this would be welcomed, especially given that now revenge pornography is a criminal offence across much of the world, it remains to be seen how such cases are discussed in a court setting.

Sex differences also play a core role in victim blaming, with men being significantly more likely to place blame than women in instances of IBSA (Bothamley & Tully, 2018; Fido et al., 2022)—a finding which is consistent with a wider range of sexual offences (McCaul et al., 1990). Though this is likely an artefact of an experiential component in which women might have heightened awareness of the inherent risks involved in making and sharing private sexual images, this does suggest a lack of broader education around the role of sharing images in normative relationship formation and associated stigmas in contexts where this results in IBSA.

Conclusions

Taken together, this chapter has sought to not only conceptualise and define the constellation of image-based sexual abuses (revenge pornography, upskirting, deepfake media production, and cyber-flashing) but has also begun to introduce some of the core discussion points and topics of required investigation in this ever-important area of forensic psychology. Specifically, it acts as a call to arms for stakeholders across legal, psychological, and education spheres to work together to further develop this corpus of knowledge. Technology advances at a rate that makes it nearly impossible for lawmakers to keep up with, and so frequent consultations and collaborations are required to combat this—especially in victim-focused areas; such as identifying barriers to reporting and better understanding the experiences of victims once they enter the criminal justice system and longitudinally throughout their lives thereafter.

References

Japan Gazette (October 2, 2020). Adult video creation with "Deep Fake" technology or first arrest. *Japan Gazette.* https://japangazette.com/2020/10/02/adult-video-creation-with-deep-fake-technology-or-first-arrest/

Arnocky, S., & Vaillancourt, T. (2017). Sexual competition among women: A review of the theory and supporting evidence. In M. L. Fisher (Ed.), *The Oxford handbook of women and competition* (pp. 25–39). Oxford University Press.

Beech, A. R., & Mann, R. E. (2002). Recent developments in the assessment and treatment of sexual offenders. In J. Maguire (Ed.), Offender rehabilitation and treatment: *Effective programmes and policies to reduce re-offending* 259–288. Wiley.

Blake, K. R., Bastian, B., Denson, T. F., Grosjean, P., & Brooks, R. C. (2018). Income inequality not gender inequality positively covaries with female sexualisation on social media. *Proceedings of the National Academy of Sciences of the United States of America, 115*, 8722–8727.

Bothamley, S., & Tully, R. J. (2018). Understanding revenge pornography: Public perceptions of revenge pornography and victim blaming. *Journal of Aggression, Conflict and Peace Research, 10*, 1–10.

Burt, M. R. (1980). Cultural myths and supports for rape. *Journal of Personality and Social Psychology, 38*, 217–230.

Dawkins, J. T. (2015). A dish served cold: The case for criminalizing revenge pornography. *Cumberland Law Review, 45*, 395–447.

Delfino, R. (2019). Pornographic deepfakes: The case for federal criminalization of revenge porn's next tragic act. *Actual Problems of Economics and Law, 14*, 887–938.

Drouin, M., & Landgraff, C. (2012). Texting, sexting, and attachment in college students' romantic relationships. *Computers in Human Behavior, 28*, 444–449.

Dubbs, S. L., Kelly, A. J., & Barlow, F. K. (2017). *Ravishing rivals: Female intrasexual competition and cosmetic surgery.* In M. L. Fisher (Ed.), *Oxford library of psychology. The Oxford handbook of women and competition* (pp. 597–615). Oxford University Press.

Fay, M. (2018). The naked truth: Insufficient coverage for revenge porn victims at state law and the proposed federal legislation to adequately redress them. *Boston College Law Review, 59*, 1839–1871.

Fido, D., Harper, C. A., Davis, M., Petronzi, D., & Worrall, S. G. M. (2021). Intrasexual competition as a predictor of women's judgements of revenge pornography offending. *Sexual Abuse, 33*(3), 295–320.

Fido, D., Harper, C. A., Duff, S., & Page, T. E. (2025) Understanding social judgments of and proclivities to commit upskirting. *Sexual Abuse, 37*(3), 339–367. https://doi.org/10.1177/10790632241268469

Fido, D., Rao, J., & Harper, C. (2022). Understanding judgements and attitudes towards deepfake media production. *Computers in Human Behavior, 129*, Article 107141.

Fido, D., & Harper, C. A. (2020). *Non-consensual image-based sexual offending: Bridging legal and psychological perspectives.* Palgrave.

Fido, D., Harper, C. A., Davis, .A., Petronzi,D., & Worrall,S. (2021). Intrasexual competition as a predictor of women's judgments of revenge pornography offending *Sexual Abuse 33*(3) 295–320. https://doi.org/10.1177/1079063219894306

Field, T., Diego, M., Pelaez, M., Deeds, O., & Delgado, J. (2009). Break-up distress in university students. *Adolescence, 44*, 705–727.

Figueredo, A. J., Cabeza de Baca, T., & Woodley, M. A. (2013). The measurement of human life history strategy. *Personality and Individual Differences, 55*, 251–255.

Garcia, J. R., Reiber, C., Massey, S. G., & Merriweather, A. M. (2012). Sexual hookup culture: A review. *Review of General Psychology, 16*, 161–176.

Griskevicius, V., Tybur, J. M., Sundie, J. M., Cialdini, R. B., Miller, G. F., & Kenrick, D. T. (2007). Blatant benevolence and conspicuous consumption: When romantic motives elicit strategic costly signals. *Journal of Personality and Social Psychology, 93*, 85–102.

Hall, M., & Hearn, J. (2018). *Revenge pornography: Gender, sexualities and motivations.* Routledge.

Hall, M., & Hearn, J. (2019). Revenge pornography and manhood acts: A discourse analysis of perpetrators' accounts. *Journal of Gender Studies, 28*, 158–170.

Hall, M., Hearn, J., & Lewis, R. (2022). *Digital Gender-Sexual Violations*. Routledge.

Harper, C. A., Fido, D., & Petronzi, D. (2021). Delineating non-consensual sexual image offending: Towards an empirical approach. *Aggression and Violent Behavior, 58*, Article 101547.

Harper, C. A., Smith, L., & Fido, D. (2022). Development and validation of the Revenge porn Myth Scale. *Sexual Abuse* [online first] https://doi.org/10.1177/10790632221082663

Henry, N., & Powell, A. (2015a). Beyond the 'sext': Technology-facilitated sexual violence and harassment against adult women. *Australian & New Zealand Journal of Criminology, 48*, 104–118.

Henry, N., & Powell, A. (2015b). Embodied harms: Gender, shame, and technology-facilitated sexual violence. *Violence against Women, 21*, 758–779.

Henry, N., & Powell, A. (2016). Sexual violence in the digital age: The scope and limits of criminal law. *Social & Legal Studies, 25*, 397–418.

Henry, N., Powell, A., & Flynn, A. (2017). *Not just 'revenge pornography': Australians' experiences of image-based abuse*. RMIT University.

Hickey, K. (2018). Using technology to impede privacy and consent: A survey of revenge porn laws. *American Criminal Law Review*, 55.

Howells, K., Day, A., & Wright, S. (2004). Affect, emotions, and sex offending. *Psychology, Crime & Law, 10*(2), 179–195.

Jonason, P. K., & Kavanagh, P. (2010). The dark side of love: The Dark Triad and love styles. *Personality and Individual Differences, 49*, 606–610.

Jonason, P. K., Li, N. P., Webster, G. W., & Schmitt, D. P. (2009). The Dark Triad: Facilitating short-term mating in men. *European Journal of Personality, 23*, 5–18.

Jonason, P. K., Webster, G. W., Schmitt, D. P., Li, N. P., & Crysel, L. (2012). The antihero in popular culture: A life history theory of the Dark Triad. *Review of General Psychology, 16*, 192–199.

Långström, N., & Seto, M. C. (2006) Exhibitionistic and voyeuristic behavior in a Swedish national population survey. *Archives of Sexual Behavior*, *35*(4), 427–435. https://doi.org/10.1007/s10508-006-9042-6

Lichter, S. (2013, May 28). Unwanted exposure: civil and criminal liability for revenge porn hosts and posters. *JOLT Digest: Harvard Journal of Law and Technology*. Retrieved from http://jolt.law.harvard.edu/dig est/ privacy/unwanted-exposure-civil-and-criminal-liability-for-revenge-porn-hosts-and-posters.

Mann, R., & Smith, L. (2020). *Revenge pornography: Does a victim's online portrayal impact perceptions of victim blame, victim harm and the extent to which it is viewed to be a crime?* Manuscript in preparation.

McCaul, K. D., Veltum, L. G., Boyechko, V., & Crawford, J. J. (1990). Understanding attributions of victim blame for rape: Sex, violence, and foreseeability. *Journal of Applied Social Psychology, 20*, 1–26.

McGlynn, C., Rackley, E., & Houghton, R. (2017). Beyond 'revenge porn': The continuum of image-based sexual abuse. *Feminist Legal Studies, 25*, 25–46.

McManus, M. A., Hargreaves, P., Rainbow, L., & Alison, L. (2013). Paraphilias: Definition, diagnosis and treatment. *F1000Prime Reports, 5*, 36–42.

Pemberton, A. E., & Wakeling, H. C. (2009). Entitled to sex: Attitudes of sexual offenders. *Journal of Sexual Aggression, 15*, 289–303.

Quayle, E., & Taylor, M. (2002). Child pornography and the Internet: Perpetuating a cycle of abuse. *Deviant Behavior, 23*, 331–361.

Rofer, J. (2016). Nonconsensual pornography: An old crime updates its software. *Fordham Intellectual Property, Media and Entertainment Law, 27*, 935.

Seto, M. C. (2019). The motivation-facilitation model of sexual offending. *Sexual Abuse, 31*, 3–24.

Stroud, S. R. (2014). The dark side of the online self: A pragmatist critique of the growing plague of revenge porn. *Journal of Mass Media Ethics, 29*, 168–183.

Thompson, R. (2019, Jul 19). It's time to stop saying 'unsolicited dick pics.' Here's why. *Mashable*. Retrieved from: https://mashable.com/article/cyberflashing-unsolicited-dick-pics-terminology/?europe=true.

Visser, J. (2012, April 20). Isanyoneup.com, revenge porn website, shuts down after selling to anti-bullying group. *National Post*. Retrieved from: https://nationalpost.com/news/isanyoneup-com-revenge-porn-website-shuts-down-after-selling-to-anti-bullying-group.

Waling, A., & Pym, T. (2019). 'C'mon, no one wants a dick pic': Exploring the cultural framings of the 'dick pic' in contemporary online publics. *Journal of Gender Studies, 28*, 70–85.

Walton, M. T., Cantor, J. M., Bhullar, N., & Lykins, A. D. (2017). Hypersexuality: A critical review and introduction to the "sexhavior cycle." *Archives of Sexual Behavior, 46*, 2231–2251.

Ward, T., & Beach, A.(2006) An integrated theory of sexual offending. *Aggression and Violent Behavior, 11*(1), 44–63. https://doi.org/10.1016/j.avb.2005.05.002

Ward, T., & Beech, A. R. (2016). The integrated theory of sexual offending–revised: A multifield perspective. *The Wiley handbook on the theories, assessment and treatment of sexual offending*, 123–137.

Ward, T., & Siegert, R. J. (2002). Toward a comprehensive theory of child sexual abuse: A theory knitting perspective. *Psychology, Crime & Law, 8*(4), 319–351.

Williams, K. M., Cooper, B. S., Howell, T. M., Yuille, J. C., & Paulhus, D. L. (2009). Inferring sexually deviant behavior from corresponding fantasies: The role of personality and pornography consumption. *Criminal Justice and Behavior, 36*, 198–222.

Wright, M. F., Harper, B. D., & Wachs, S. (2019). The associations between cyberbullying and callous-unemotional traits among adolescents: The moderating effect of online disinhibition. *Personality and Individual Differences, 140*, 41–45.

CHAPTER 5

When Swiping Goes Wrong: Dating Applications, Interpersonal Aggression, and Sexual Violence

Brandon Sparks and Rebecca Fisico

Introduction

The rise of internet use and smartphone ownership has profoundly impacted the social, economic, and political landscapes in the US and abroad, with one corresponding shift being the way romantic relationships are formed. Indeed, by 2013, for the first time in nearly 60 years, the dominant role friends played in the initiation of relationships began to plummet, with this decline seemingly being attributable to the skyrocketing proportion of people meeting their romantic partners online (Rosenfeld et al., 2019). This dramatic movement toward technology-facilitated dating experienced two main periods of growth.

B. Sparks (✉)
University of New Brunswick, Saint John, Canada
e-mail: bsparks@unb.ca

R. Fisico
McMaster University, Hamilton, Canada
e-mail: fisicor@mcmaster.ca

C. A. Harper et al. (eds.), *Sexual Crime and the Internet*, Sexual Crime,
https://doi.org/10.1007/978-3-031-95844-1_5

The first occurred during the mid-1990s to mid-2000s, when many dating websites such as Match, eHarmony, and Plenty of Fish went online. The second began around 2010, coinciding with the upsurge in the number of people using mobile dating applications such as Tinder, Bumble, and (later) Hinge. In fact, Rosenfeld and colleagues (2019) report that dating applications contributed to at least half of the growth in technology-facilitated dating between 2010 and 2017.

In contrast to the old-school algorithms that sought to match users based on their responses to lengthy questionnaires, a hallmark of the online dating site eHarmony, many dating applications show their users all potential matches within their age, distance, and gender parameters (Gabbatiss, 2018; Ranzini & Lutz, 2017). After dating application users build their profile, they can begin to view profiles of users in their area and indicate their interest in different ways (e.g., swiping), depending on an online platform's interface (Choi et al., 2018; Fansher & McCarns, 2019; Murphy, 2017). Although there are different mechanisms for showing interest in a fellow user, the swiping feature is common across multiple popular platforms, with right and left swipes reflecting interest and disinterest, respectively. If two individuals indicate mutual interest in one another, they "match" and are granted the ability to engage with each other directly, often through an online chat (see Fig. 5.1). Despite this process being common, some dating applications have unique parameters. For example, on the "feminist dating application" Bumble, in matches that occur between men and women, only the women can initiate conversations upon matching (Bumble, 2021). It is notable that not all dating applications use a matching process. For instance, Grindr, a dating application that caters to the gay and men who have sex with men (MSM) community allows users within a set location radius to message one another without a mutual selection, like traditional online dating websites (Wang et al., 2018).

A. First, users are presented a profile of another user. When first shown a profile, users are typically presented with one picture, the age and the proximity of the other user. In this example, the user was presented with Jason's profile.

B. Users are then able to scroll or click through additional information the other user chose to include on their profile (e.g., biographies, pictures, likes and dislikes). In this example, Jason included a biography about himself.

C. Users can then indicate interest or disinterest in the profile they are viewing by swiping in the appropriate direction (i.e., right = interest, left

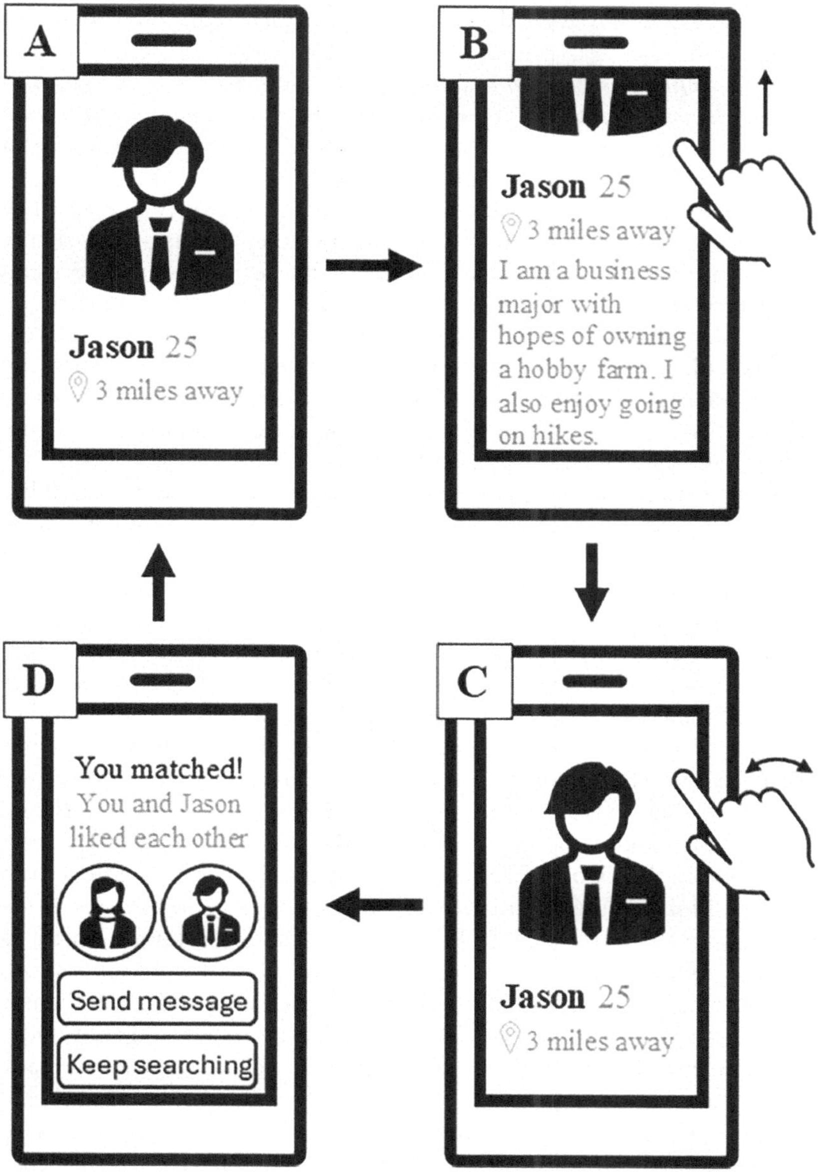

Fig. 5.1 Flow of dating app use

= disinterest). In this example, the user swiped right, suggesting interest in Jason.

D. Following this decision-making process, users are either shown more users or are notified that they have "matched" with the person and the option to initiate a conversation is presented. In this example, Jason had indicated mutual interest in the user, which resulted in a "match."

Not only are dating applications growing in popularity overall, they have become particularly trendy among younger adults. In a survey conducted by the Pew Research Center, 18–24-year-olds reported using dating applications at the highest rate when compared to the other age groups examined, with one in five reporting lifetime usage (Smith, 2016a, 2016b). Other studies have found that dating applications are particularly popular among college students (Boillot Fansher, 2017), and to possibly cater to this demographic, many traditional dating websites (e.g., Plenty of Fish, OkCupid) have developed dating applications of their own.

The growth in dating application popularity may be due to a number of features and characteristics that are not present in online dating predecessors. For example, dating applications are more accessible than computer-based dating platforms, as they are available on mobile devices (Ranzini & Lutz, 2017). Dating applications are also affordable, as many are free to use, but users can purchase optional upgrades (Schrock, 2015). Dating application users also can engage with different forms of media, as some applications allow users to send pictures and videos to one another (Schrock, 2015). Another convenient feature of many dating applications is their ability to link to users' social media accounts (e.g., Facebook) and use them to help build their dating profile (Fansher & Eckinger, 2021). Dating applications, such as Tinder, Bumble, and Hinge, also let users choose whom they would like to interact with online, which differs from many traditional dating websites where users were able to message virtually any other user (Couch & Liamputtong, 2008). Another benefit is that the common swiping and matching process of dating applications was designed to feel "game-like" to facilitate enjoyment and maintain user engagement (Stampler, 2014). Considering these enticing and convenient features, it may be unsurprising why dating applications appeal to many people.

Although they are referred to as *dating* applications, researchers have identified various motives for using these online platforms, with it being common for users to endorse more than one motive (Sawyer et al.,

2018; Sumter et al., 2017; Timmermans & De Caluwé, 2017). Timmermans and De Caluwé (2017) list 13 potential reasons for using dating applications in their Tinder Motives Scale. Among these 13 reasons, entertainment and curiosity were the most strongly endorsed motives, and the motives of belongingness and getting over a former partner were the least common. Sumter and colleagues (2017) also assessed people's motives for using the dating application Tinder, across six domains and found that the two most highly endorsed motivations were excitement and trendiness. Moreover, seeking love and enhancing one's self-worth were more strongly endorsed than casual sex and ease of communication. These findings suggest that dating applications may be a misnomer in many cases, as they are used for a variety of reasons, beyond those related to relationship initiation.

Dating Application-Facilitated Violence

Although dating applications have become a commonplace means to develop new sought-after connections, there is growing recognition that dating applications are also acting as new avenues for traditional forms of abuse to take place (Hess & Flores, 2018) and new forms of abuse to emerge (Vitis & Gilmour, 2017). The remainder of this chapter will explore various forms of aggression and violence associated with or facilitated by dating applications, how users protect themselves, and features of dating applications that may increase user risk.

Online Violence

One form of violence dating application users report experiencing online is harassment. Duggan (2014) found that 6% of their respondents' most recent experience of online harassment took place on a dating application or dating website. Although, notably, this relatively low percentage likely underestimates dating applications' role in online harassment, as users often exchange contact information such as phone numbers and social media information shortly after "matching" (Fansher & McCarns, 2019), where much of the online harassment reportedly took place (Duggan, 2014). Despite the majority of respondents in Duggan (2014) indicating that dating applications were welcoming to both men and women, other research suggests that women may be at a heightened risk of experiencing harassment on dating applications than men. For instance, in a poll conducted by Consumers' Research, 57% of women reported having experienced some form of harassment via dating applications, compared to 21% of men (Burgess, 2016). Moreover, a larger study by Smith and Duggan (2013) found a similar gender divide among dating application and website users, with 42% of women and 15% of men reporting having been harassed or made uncomfortable by another user.

To further demonstrate the gender divide of negative experiences on dating applications, Farvid and Aisher (2016) interviewed women about their experiences on dating applications and found that many had faced aggressive responses from men after they had expressed no longer being interested in them. This pattern of male aggression toward females following rejection has also been documented in laboratory settings (e.g., Blake et al., 2018) and online through Instagram accounts such as *Tinder Nightmares* and *Bye Felipe* (Shaw, 2016; Thompson, 2018). These Instagram accounts serve as spaces for women[1] to upload screenshots of aggressive conversations that they have had with men, often on dating applications (Shaw, 2016; Thompson, 2018; Tweten, 2014). When the *rejection* and *ignore* threads of the *Bye Felipe* Instagram account were analysed, Shaw (2016) found that the threats of violent action—ranging from "petulant insults to explicit threat" (p. 5)—were present in both circumstances, with numerous commenters expressing that they or their friends have experienced similar vitriol from men who they have either rejected or ignored. In a discursive analysis of 526 posts on both the *Bye Felipe* and *Tinder Nightmares* Instagram accounts, Thompson (2018) found the most frequently documented response to a female ignoring or rejecting male advances was an attack on the female's appearance. In a survey of 324 dating application users, such degrading comments were one of the most common forms of cybervictimization reported, with roughly one-third of respondents having experienced at least one instance of emotional abuse in the past 12 months (Centelles, 2019). The experiences outlined in Centelles (2019), Shaw (2016), and Thompson (2018) were also echoed by the participants interviewed by Lopes and Vogel (2017), who felt that dating applications might be promoting these aggressive behaviours and attitudes. These findings suggest that dating applications may act as a hub for toxic misogynistic behaviours.

[1] The Instagram account *Tinder Nightmares* is not exclusive to women; however, the majority of posts are submitted by women who are documenting aggression and abuse by men (Thompson, 2018).

One of the lesser documented forms of victimization associated with dating applications is cyberstalking. Brown (2016) details an interview with Chloe (a pseudonym), who discusses her experience of being stalked by a man she had matched with on Tinder. Chloe described experiencing an escalation of disconcerting behaviour from the man. He started by asking her invasive personal questions, then sent her a friend request and numerous messages on Facebook after she had blocked him on Tinder, and finally he began physically stalking her with the aid of an application called Happn. Happn is often branded as a dating application (Happn, 2021) and it alerts users to other users in their vicinity. Emerging research suggests that Chloe's experience is not uncommon. For instance, in a sample of 324 dating application users, cyberstalking was the most commonly reported form of victimization, with almost two-thirds of participants reporting experiencing cyberstalking victimization at least once (Centelles, 2019). Specifically, 65% of respondents had been repeatedly messaged by a fellow user after they had stopped responding, one-quarter continued to receive messages after asking the person to stop, and roughly half had been contacted by a person through social media despite not providing them with their account information. Interestingly, using an equally liberal definition of cyberstalking, in another study conducted with an undergraduate sample, only 7% of dating application users reported experiencing this type of victimization (Fansher & McCarns, 2019). Given the discrepancy and lack of literature on this topic, it is imperative that future studies further investigate dating application users' experiences with cyberstalking and the potential link between cyberstalking, physical stalking, and other aggressive acts.

Offline Violence

A recent scoping review found that dating application users—especially women—expressed concern that the use of these applications may put them in an unsafe situation or increase their likelihood of being stalked (Filice et al., 2022). Similarly, MSM also worry about their physical safety while using dating applications (Steele et al., 2025). Such fears are not unjustified as over the past decade, there have been several accounts when in-person meetings facilitated by dating applications have turned lethal which have included instances of strangulation (BBC, 2020; Steinbuch, 2020), choking and stabbing (Li, 2020), and luring and dismemberment (Sokmensuer, 2020). Although these stories are among the more sensational, they highlight the seemingly growing number of people experiencing dating application-facilitated violence in person. For example, Centelles (2019) found that despite reports of online rather than in-person victimization being more common, 40% of their respondents reported experiencing at least one form of in-person violence from someone they had met on a dating application. Particularly, the most common form of in-person violence reported was emotional or verbal abuse, which was experienced by roughly one-third of the sample, followed by stalking (15%) and physical violence (5%). This suggests that the extent of dating application-facilitated violence may be underestimated by researchers and law enforcement. Respondents in Fansher and McCarns (2019) reported fewer instances of in-person violence, with 5% having been stalked offline by a person they had met through a dating application. These preliminary studies suggest that dating application users may be at risk of physical violence when meeting matches in person. However, additional research must be conducted to determine how far-reaching experiences of this nature are.

Dating Applications and Sexual Violence

Online Violence

Research suggests that dating applications have become a hotspot for technology-facilitated sexual violence, with sexual harassment emerging as one of the more prominent forms. This technological shift has been so notable that research teams have begun to modify traditional measures of sexual harassment to capture how this form of victimization occurs online. For instance, Smith (2016a, 2016b) used a pilot study to modify the Sexual Experience Questionnaire (Fitzgerald et al., 1995) to reflect online scenarios by removing items related to in-person interactions (e.g., items relating to touch) and adding technology-specific items, such as requests for explicit media and repeated aggressive messages. Using this updated measure, a follow-up study of 319 men and women found that over 90% of participants reported being a victim of sexual harassment on an online dating platform (Smith, 2016a, 2016b). Similarly, in a subsample of 535 dating application users, over half (57%) of participants reported being sexually harassed on a dating application within the past year, with 23% of participants experiencing this form of victimization "monthly or more" (Douglass et al., 2018). Studies have also suggested that the extent to which individuals use dating applications can influence the extent to which they experience sexual harassment, such that people who use dating applications more frequently report higher rates of sexual harassment (Leinung, 2019).

The experience of sexual harassment, threats, and degradation are also present in the *Bye Felipe* and *Tinder Nightmares* Instagram accounts described above. In one instance, in a post showing a circumstance where after a man's sexual advance was rejected, the man sent several messages explicitly stating that they did not care if they were interested or not (Shaw, 2016). This post prompted Instagram commenters to discuss the man's sexual entitlement, lack of respect for consent, and potential criminality. In Thompson's (2018) analysis of the two Instagram accounts, the (presumably male) dating application users were even more vulgar in describing proposed sexual encounters with their female matches, often explicitly demanding these acts. Other issues that emerged included descriptions of imagined non-consensual sexual interactions, devaluing women, and women being positioned as "deserving of harassment" (p. 83). In the *Tinder Nightmares* posts analysed by Hess and Flores (2018), similar crass comments were found. According to females in Gillett (2019), such unsolicited sexual messages from males often constitute as the first message(s) between the two, with no further substantiation. These findings insinuate that some dating application users view these online platforms as an anarchist space, whereby they can abuse other (generally female) users without consequence or any expectation of better behaviour.

One behaviour that has gained traction as constituting a form of sexual harassment or abuse is sending unsolicited sexual images, also known as "cyberflashing" (Hayes & Dragiewicz, 2018; Waling & Pym, 2017). Cyberflashing entails transmitting a sexually explicit image or video to a non-consenting person using technology. Scholars have discussed that dating applications have become one online platform where this non-consensual sexual exchange has become rampant (Shaw, 2016; Thompson, 2018; Tweten, 2014; see Hayes & Dragiewicz, 2018 for a discussion). This proposition has been supported empirically, as in a sample of U.S. adults, 35% of participants reported that they had been sent an unsolicited sexual message or image on a dating application or website (Anderson et al., 2020). Other statistics, though not specific to transmission over dating applications indicate cyberflashing is a prevalent phenomenon. For example, roughly half of the female and MSM respondents in Marcotte et al. (2021) reported having been sent a picture of a man's genitals, and within this subsample, an overwhelming majority (90%) had received an unsolicited image of this nature. Moreover, in another study, one-third of dating application users reported having been cyberflashed in the past 12 months (Centelles, 2019). Further suggesting that cyberflashing on dating applications is a commonplace experience, dating applications have begun to use artificial intelligence filters to blur images that may contain graphic content, providing users with the ability to choose whether they view the image or not (Carson, 2019). The problematic nature of cyberflashing has begun to be recognized in the legal sphere with legislation being passed to address this behaviour. In March 2022, the United Kingdom criminalized cyberflashing, being the first country to explicitly make this a criminal offence (although Scotland has recognized this for over a decade; Huet, 2022). California and Texas have also introduced cyberflashing laws, with Bumble contributing to the latter state's legislative changes (NBC, 2022; North, 2019).

It is important to note that not all sexual images are unwelcome. In fact, the sharing of an intimate image of oneself with a current or prospective sexual partner is growing increasingly common as a part of the larger practice of sexting—the sending of sexual messages and other media between consenting parties—which has itself emerged as part of larger sexual scripts (Benotsch et al., 2013; Klettke et al., 2014; Lippman & Campbell, 2014; Mori et al., 2020; Ruvalcaba et al., 2020). As dating applications are used for romantic and sexual purposes by individuals with more liberal sexual attitudes (Sevi et al., 2018; Tomaszewska & Schuster, 2020), it is likely that this practice exists either in the dating application itself or through another form of communication that has been shared with a fellow dating application user. Unfortunately, in some cases, these sexual images can be weaponized by forwarding them to colleagues, leaking them online, or threatening to release them, a range of behaviours referred to as image-based sexual abuse (IBSA; Powell et al., 2018; McGlynn et al., 2020). There has been little exploration done on the role that dating applications have played in their facilitation of these acts; though, it appears that at least some forms of victimization on dating applications are a notable occurrence, with law enforcement agencies in different parts of the world, such as Canada (Tsekouras, 2021), the US (Diprizio, 2018), and the UK (Police Service of Northern Ireland, n.d.) issuing warnings to the public about people experiencing "sextortion" (i.e., the use of blackmail or threats to coerce an unwilling person to engage in sexual acts, including the creation/sharing of intimate images; Powell & Henry, 2017) through these platforms. These reports suggest that dating applications may indeed be an online platform where IBSA can occur, highlighting the need for more research to be conducted to better understand how people are experiencing and perpetrating IBSA through dating applications.

Offline Violence

The risk of sexual violence for dating application users extends beyond the screen. Filice et al.'s (2022) scoping review found that the proportion of dating application users who experienced sexual violence or aggression through someone met on the application ranged from roughly one in ten to one in three people depending on the population and definitions used. Indeed, emerging research does suggest that dating application users may be at an increased risk for in-person sexual violence. For example, a survey conducted with a sample of university students in Hong Kong found that dating application users were 2.13 times more likely to have experienced sexual abuse and 2.09 times more likely to have been forced to have unprotected sex in the past year compared to non-users (Choi et al., 2018). Shapiro et al. (2017) found that Tinder users were three times as likely to report experiencing non-consensual sex than non-users. In Snaychuk and O'Neill (2020), one-quarter of women and 10% of men reported an unwanted sexual experience with someone they had met via a dating application or website. Although these studies do not unequivocally identify dating applications as facilitators of in-person sexual violence, police report data have demonstrated quite damning evidence for a link between these online platforms and in-person sexual violence. For instance, based on data collected from police services in the UK, the National Crime Agency (NCA, 2016) reported that the rate of sexual offences involving dating applications or websites had increased six-fold between 2009 and 2014. Between 2003 and 2015, over half of the victims were under the age of 30 (NCA, 2016), in line with user demographics (Smith, 2016a, 2016b). Victims were also predominantly (85%) female with three-quarters of offences taking place at a residence (NCA, 2016).

These findings were echoed by Rowse et al. (2020) in their analysis of case files from a clinical forensic medical service in Australia, which provides further evidence of a link between dating applications and experiencing in-person sexual assault. Specifically, of the 76 sexual assault reports examined, 15% of victims reported having met the accused on a dating application. In all instances, this was a female victim reporting a male assailant. Most often, the assault occurred on the first date and involved some sort of impairment (e.g., alcohol intoxication, illicit drug use). Additionally, two cases concerned individuals with an intellectual disability who lived in a residential care facility. This finding suggests that although it is important for researchers and developers to identify additional strategies to ensure that all users can safely navigate dating applications, it is also imperative that special consideration is given to determine how to keep potentially more vulnerable populations using these applications safe, as there are several. For instance, trans-dating application users report that some of the safety issues they face when using dating applications are infrequently acknowledged by cis users (Albury et al., 2021). Dangers in disclosing their trans identity and exposure to transphobic messages and profiles were among some of the more prominent concerns described. Others reported that their gender non-confirmation was fetishized by other users and expressed discomfort in being pursued exclusively for that reason (Albury et al., 2021).

A reliance on police-report data, while useful, poses its own problems, especially as it relates to the reporting of sexual assault. Some estimates suggest that three quarters of sexual assaults are not reported to police (Department of Justice, 2017). Thus, like other forms of sexual violence, getting an accurate picture of the role that dating applications play in the facilitation of sexual assault is difficult, as each methodological approach invites unique advantages and limitations. Although media coverage does not offer exhaustive or necessarily representative accounts, like empirical research, they have also identified dating application-facilitated sexual assaults as an emerging issue. In Dias et al. (2020a)'s investigation of dating application safety, 48 of the 231 Tinder users surveyed were sexually victimized by someone they had met on Tinder and reported their experience to the dating application, with less than a quarter receiving a response to their report. Dias et al.'s (2020a) report also highlighted the case of Glenn Hartland or "the Tinder Rapist," who was found to have committed a string of sexual offences against women that he had met on the dating application. This has led to calls for Tinder and other dating applications to ban individuals with sexual convictions from ever using the application (Dias, 2020; Flynn et al., 2019), akin to other petitions to ban people who have committed sexual offences from other digital platforms (Hutt, 2019; Mico, 2019). These reports further demonstrate the need for additional research to determine changes that are required to prevent this form of victimization. They also highlight the role dating applications play in responding to reports of violence to be clarified to ensure that victims feel heard rather than invalidated when they reach out and are responded to appropriately.

How Do Dating Application Users Protect Themselves?

Despite the limited literature, it appears that people are aware of the risks that dating applications may pose to users. For instance, the companies who run the dating applications (e.g., Bumble, Tinder) demonstrate awareness by posting safety tips on their websites (Bumble, 2021; Tinder, 2021). Dating application users also exhibit awareness of these risks, as many report taking precautions before meeting someone from a dating application in person. In their sample of 887 college students, Fansher and McCarns (2019) found that overall, three-quarters of dating application users had met someone offline that they had initially contacted through a dating application. Before these meetings, women reported engaging in roughly two and a half precautions, such as charging their cell phone and telling a friend about their plans or location. The number of precautions taken by women was significantly more than the average of one and a half precautions taken by men. Furthermore, only one female user reported taking no precautions, compared to 13 male users. Like Fansher and McCarns (2019), women in Albury et al. (2019)'s Australian sample reported engaging in more precautionary strategies when meeting a person from a dating application in person, such as meeting in a public place. This precaution was even practised in circumstances where dating application users aimed to engage in casual sex, as it provides people an easy "out" if they changed their mind. Also, although some females reported going immediately to a date's home, they indicated that they felt fearful when doing so. This concern for safety was more commonly reported among heterosexual, bisexual, and non-binary women who dated cis-gendered men. Notably, respondents in Albury et al. (2019)'s Australian sample indicated that they employed safety precautions even before an in-person meeting took place by screening dating application profiles and message conversations for potential "red flags." These findings suggest that users are aware of the risks dating applications pose and use strategies to protect themselves. Future research should further examine what precautionary strategies dating application users employ and what strategies appear to be most effective.

Why Dating Applications May Facilitate Violence

It is not only of interest *if* dating applications facilitate violence but also *why* they do. In short, there is no concrete answer—yet. However, there are some characteristics of dating applications and the users themselves that may provide some insight into this question.

Characteristics of Online Platforms

Online platforms, such as dating applications, possess numerous characteristics that at first blush appear inherently advantageous; however, after closer examination, some beloved features may also possess important disadvantages. For example, technology affords people the ability to connect with others with ease, regardless of time and proximity. Although this can be convenient, this ease of access can provide perpetrators with the ability to torment their victims without these restrictions (Government of Quebec, n.d.; Pooley & Boxall, 2020). Another appealing feature of online platforms, particularly those for online dating, is that they provide increased access to a seemingly unlimited number of potential partners (Finkel et al., 2012). In theory, this access to a larger dating pool is favourable as it could increase someone's odds of finding their match; however, it could also expose someone to a greater network of people who may have antisocial motives or a proclivity to engage in aggressive or harmful behaviour. An additional attractive feature of dating applications is their tendency to use location-based interfaces, as this feature may seem like an inherently convenient way of connecting with nearby matches. Although users of location-based dating applications run the risk of unintentionally disclosing their location in real time, and research suggests that many dating application users may not be aware of this risk (Fansher & McCarns, 2019).

Another apparent benefit of online platforms is that some people may feel more comfortable online. At first, this comfortability may appear positive, but according to the online disinhibition effect, these feelings online can promote "toxic disinhibition," whereby people can engage in disconcerting behaviours online (e.g., harassment, threats), that they would not offline (Suler, 2004). Suler (2004) discusses six features online platforms afford to users that appear to contribute to this process, one being "dissociative anonymity," which is arguably of particular concern on dating applications. Indeed, the freedom dating application users are provided when constructing their profile, also presents them with the opportunity to falsify their identity to make it more appealing to potential mates (Scannell, 2019). To help mitigate this potential issue, dating applications have developed mechanisms for users to verify their identities (e.g., photo verification), but these developments are novel and optional (Carman, 2020). Also, even if a person provides some legitimate personal details on their profile or within conversations, an investigation by Dias and colleagues (2020a) found that some people have discovered a new means of facilitating retroactive anonymity after engaging in an assault. Specifically, individuals can use the "unmatch" feature provided by Tinder—which erases the messages between the users and other contact information—following assaults. This erasure can seemingly serve to eliminate any evidence of the user's identity and connection to the other user, working to facilitate quasi-anonymity. While Tinder responded to the above investigation, claiming that it has updated the reporting functions and can retrieve deleted messages, they did not comment on the issues raised with the unmatch feature, which puts extra emphasis on the victim and police to contact Tinder directly to retrieve information that was previously accessible (Dias et al., 2020b).

In addition to online disinhibition having the potential to facilitate "toxic" behaviour, it also has the potential to increase people's propensity to share more intimate information with people online than they would offline, something Suler (2004) refers to as "benign disinhibition." It could then be posited that offering these details about oneself can increase someone's vulnerability to victimization, particularly when meeting in person. In line with this, in a report about dating application-facilitated sexual victimization, the NCA (2016) explained that online communications of this nature may remove any sense of stranger danger, leading people to be less cautious when meeting in person. The NCA (2016) also noted that when people feel disinhibited online, they may engage in sexual conversations which prompt expectations of in-person sexual activity. If not shared by all parties, these expectations may be troublesome, as they could contribute to the commission of offences (NCA, 2016).

Dating Application User Characteristics

Empirical research has begun to suggest that certain disconcerting or "Dark" personality characteristics are associated with using dating applications. For instance, in a sample of 271 participants from the United States, Sevi (2019a, 2019b) found that dating application users scored higher than non-users on all three Dark Triad personality traits (i.e., narcissism, psychopathy, and Machiavellianism). In this study, the Dark Triad traits were also associated with using Tinder for short-term (i.e., casual sex) purposes. Using a larger sample of 587 participants, Duncan and March (2019) found associations between the four Dark Tetrad personality traits (i.e., the Dark Triad traits plus sadism) and three antisocial uses of dating applications. Of note, all four traits were related to the use of dating applications for antisocial reasons, which included to "harass other users" and "create conflict." In contrast, three of the traits, namely Machiavellianism, psychopathy, and sadism, were related to using dating applications for sexual antisocial reasons, which included items such as using Tinder to "sexually coerce others" and "meet my own sexual needs, disregarding the benefit of others." An earlier study also linked the Dark Tetrad traits to using dating applications for the purposes of "trolling," which is an online antisocial behaviour of intentional provocation (Bishop, 2014; March et al., 2017). Paired with research linking these Dark traits to intimate partner violence (IPV; Carton & Egan, 2017), sexual coercion (Lyons et al., 2020), IBSA (Karasavva, 2020), cyberstalking (Stiff, 2019), and cyber-aggression (Pabian et al., 2015; van Geel et al., 2017), it is possible to conclude that individuals who use dating applications may possess personality characteristics that may increase a person's propensity to engage in violent behaviour, leading them to be a potentially risky online platform to use.

Conclusion

Upon reading this chapter, those who have not used dating applications may question their popularity given their risk, whereas those who have used dating applications may have reflected on their own positive and negative experiences with these online platforms. Regardless of one's level of experience with dating applications, it is likely that all readers will come away with concerns about dating application user safety. Even though reading this chapter may be jarring to people for different reasons and in different ways, we would like to highlight that this chapter's goal was not to promote fear, but instead, awareness. In a society seemingly characterized by its technological innovations, it is important for people to be aware of both sides of the technological coin. Namely, although dating applications have many advantages, such as initiating new relationships, the evidence presented in this chapter suggests that they are also platforms that can facilitate various forms of perpetration and victimization, both online and in-person. As more evidence emerges further supporting this disconcerting reality associated with dating applications, it is important that steps are taken to promote the safety of their users. Thus, this chapter also aims to encourage stakeholders who are involved in keeping dating application users safe to conduct more research, as well as develop new features and legislation (indeed, some are; see Bill SB-1182, 2020; North, 2019; Ritzau, 2018), to ensure that dating application users are protected and that their safety is more than equivalent to an outcome of chance. We also encourage stakeholders to truly listen to the experiences dating application users share, rather than look at them as anecdotal or one-off reports, recognizing that their experiences are real, deserve attention, and require a response. Ultimately, we hope that these responses to dating application-facilitated violence will begin to be proactive rather than reactive, facilitating a safer space for dating application users to swipe, match, and meet.

References

Albury, K., Byron, P., McCosker, A., Pym, T., Walshe, J., Race, K., & Dietzel, C. (2019). *Safety, risk and wellbeing on dating apps: Final report*. Swinburne University of Technology.

Albury, K., Dietzel, C., Pym, T., Vivienne, S., & Cook, T. (2021). Not your unicorn: Trans dating app users' negotiations of personal safety and sexual health. *Health Sociology Review, 30*(1), 72–86.

Anderson, M., Vogels, E., & Turner, E. (2020). *The virtues and downsides of online dating*. Pew Research Center. https://www.pewresearch.org/internet/2020/02/06/the-virtues-and-downsides-of-online-dating/

Avari, J. (2014). Alleged Grindr security flaw exposes exact location data, endangers users. *Gadgets 360*. https://gadgets.ndtv.com/apps/news/alleged-grindr-security-flaw-exposes-exact-location-data-endangers-users-1-579031

BBC. (2020). Grace Millane case: 'I went on a date with her killer after her murder.' *Author*. https://www.bbc.com/news/uk-england-essex-51563388

Benotsch, E. G., Snipes, D. J., Martin, A. M., & Bull, S. S. (2013). Sexting, substance use, and sexual risk behavior in young adults. *Journal of Adolescent Health, 52*(3), 307–313.

Bill SB-1182. (2020). *Unsolicited images.* https://leginfo.legislature.ca.gov/faces/billTextClient.xhtml?bill_id=201920200SB1182

Bishop, J. (2014). Representations of 'trolls' in mass media communication: A review of media-texts and moral panics relating to 'internet trolling.' *International Journal of Web Based CoMmunities, 10*(1), 7–24.

Blake, K. R., Bastian, B., & Denson, T. F. (2018). Heightened male aggression toward sexualized women following romantic rejection: The mediating role of sex goal activation. *Aggressive Behavior, 44*(1), 40–49.

Boillot Fansher, A. K. (2017). *Risky dating behaviors in the technological age: Consideration of a new pathway to victimization* (Doctoral dissertation). Sam Houston State University.

Brown, L. (2016). I was stalked by someone I met on Tinder. *The Tab.* https://thetab.com/uk/york/2016/05/12/i-stalked-someone-i-met-tinder-10249?cmpredirect

Bumble. (2021). Bumble. https://bumble.com/

Burgess, K. (2016). Consumer survey: The best way to "swipe" a mate. *Consumers' Research.* http://consumersresearch.org/consumer-survey-the-best-way-to-swipe-a-mate/

Carman, A. (2020). Tinder will give you a verified blue check mark if you pass its catfishing test. *The Verge.* https://www.theverge.com/2020/1/23/21077423/tinder-photo-verification-blue-checkmark-safety-center-launch-noonlight

Carson, E. (2019). Bumble will use AI to protect you from unwanted dick pics. *CNet.* https://www.cnet.com/news/bumble-will-use-ai-to-protect-you-from-unwanted-dick-pics/

Carton, H., & Egan, V. (2017). The dark triad and intimate partner violence. *Personality and Individual Differences, 105*, 84–88.

Centelles, V. (2019). *Dating application facilitated victimization: An examination of lifestyle-routine activities, self-control, and self-efficacy* (Master's thesis). University of South Florida.

Choi, E. P. H., Wong, J. Y. H., & Fong, D. Y. T. (2018). An emerging risk factor of sexual abuse: The use of smartphone dating applications. *Sexual Abuse, 30*(4), 343–366.

Choi, E. P. H., Wong, J. Y. H., Lo, H. H. M., Wong, W., Chio, J. H. M., & Fong, D. Y. T. (2016). The impacts of using smartphone dating applications on sexual risk behaviours in college students in Hong Kong. *PLoS ONE, 11*(11), Article e0165394.

Choi, E. P., Wong, J. Y., Lo, H. H., Wong, W., Chio, J. H., & Fong, D. Y. (2017). Association between using smartphone dating applications and alcohol and recreational drug use in conjunction with sexual activities in college students. *Substance Use & Misuse, 52*(4), 422–428.

Ciocca, G., Robilotta, A., Fontanesi, L., Sansone, A., D'Antuono, L., Limoncin, E., & Jannini, E. A. (2020). Sexological aspects related to Tinder use: A comprehensive review of the literature. *Sexual Medicine Reviews*, advance online copy.

Couch, D., & Liamputtong, P. (2008). Online dating and mating: The use of the internet to meet sexual partners. *Qualitative Health Research, 18*(2), 268–279.

CTV News. (2016). Are dating apps really to blame for spikes in sexually transmitted diseases? *Author*. https://www.ctvnews.ca/health/are-dating-apps-really-to-blame-for-spikes-in-sexually-transmitted-diseases-1.2882367

Department of Justice. (2017). *National crime victimization survey, 2010–2016.* Bureau of Justice Statistics.

Dewey, C. (2014). Do dating apps have a prostitution problem? *The Washington Post*. https://www.washingtonpost.com/news/the-intersect/wp/2014/07/21/do-dating-apps-have-a-prostitution-problem/

Dias, A. (2020). Parents of woman sexually assaulted by Tinder rapist Glenn Hartland say app should stop serial offenders. *ABC*. https://www.abc.net.au/news/2020-10-13/tinder-rapist-glenn-hartland-used-fake-profiles-to-lure-women/12742670

Dias, A., McCormack, A., & Russell, A. (2020a). Unmatched. *ABC*. https://www.abc.net.au/news/2020-10-12/tinder-dating-app-helps-sexual-predators-hide-four-corners/12722732?nw=0

Dias, A., McCormack, A., & Russell, A. (2020b). Match Group changes Tinder's safety policies following four corners and hack investigation. *ABC*. https://www.abc.net.au/triplej/programs/hack/match-group-makes-changes-to-apps-safety-policies-following-fou/12778794

Diprizio, J. (2018). Avoiding the "sextortion trap" when online dating. *Local 24*. https://www.localmemphis.com/article/news/local/avoiding-the-sextortion-trap-when-online-dating/522-1ad82562-7aff-47bc-a0f1-d7035580ef9d

Douglass, C. H., Wright, C. J., Davis, A. C., & Lim, M. S. (2018). Correlates of in-person and technology-facilitated sexual harassment from an online survey among young Australians. *Sexual Health, 15*(4), 361–365.

Duggan, M. (2014). *Online harassment*. Pew Research Center. https://www.pewresearch.org/internet/2014/10/22/online-harassment/

Duncan, Z., & March, E. (2019). Using Tinder® to start a fire: Predicting antisocial use of Tinder® with gender and the Dark Tetrad. *Personality and Individual Differences, 145*, 9–14.

Fansher, A. K., & Eckinger, S. (2021). Tinder tales: An exploratory study of online dating users and their most interesting stories. *Deviant Behavior, 42*(9), 1194–1208.

Fansher, A. K., & McCarns, K. (2019). *Risky online dating behaviors and their potential for victimization*. Sam Houston State University.
Farvid, P., & Aisher, K. (2016). 'It's just a lot more casual': Young heterosexual women's experience of using Tinder in New Zealand. *Ada: A Journal of Gender, New Media, and Technology, 10*
Filice, E., Abeywickrama, K. D., Parry, D. C., & Johnson, C. W. (2022). Sexual violence and abuse in online dating: A scoping review. *Aggression and Violent Behavior*, 101781.
Finkel, E. J., Eastwick, P. W., Karney, B. R., Reis, H. T., & Sprecher, S. (2012). Online dating: A critical analysis from the perspective of psychological science. *Psychological Science in the Public Interest, 13*(1), 3–66.
Fitzgerald, L. F., Gelfand, M. J., & Drasgow, F. (1995). Measuring sexual harassment: Theoretical and psychometric advances. *Basic and Applied Social Psychology, 17*(4), 425–445.
Flynn, H., Cousin, K., & Picciani, E. N. (2019). Tinder lets known sex offenders use the App. It's not the only one. *ProPublica*. https://www.propublica.org/article/tinder-lets-known-sex-offenders-use-the-app-its-not-the-only-one
Gabbatiss, J. (2018). eHarmony banned from claiming dating site's matching system is 'scientifically proven.' *The Independent*. http://independent.co.uk/news/science/eharmony-dating-sitescientifically-proven-not-banned-advertising-matching-system-science-a8139201.html
Gillett, R. (2019). *Everyday violence: Women's experiences of intimate intrusions on Tinder* (Doctoral dissertation). Queensland University of Technology.
Government of Quebec. (n.d.). *Online violence: Let's work on it together*. Author.
Happn. (2021). Happn. https://www.happn.com/en/
Hayes, R. M., & Dragiewicz, M. (2018). Unsolicited dick pics: Erotica, exhibitionism or entitlement? *Women's Studies International Forum, 71*, 114–120.
Hess, A., & Flores, C. (2018). Simply more than swiping left: A critical analysis of toxic masculine performances on Tinder Nightmares. *New Media & Society, 20*(3), 1085–1102.
Hopkins, S. (2016). Crimes linked to Tinder and Grindr jum sevenfold in two years, with violence and sex offending most common. *Huffington Post*. https://www.huffingtonpost.co.uk/2016/01/11/tinder-and-grindr-crimes-jump-sevenfold-in-two-years_n_8952356.html
Huet, N. (2022). The UK is introducing a "cyberflashing" law that makes sending unsolicited "dick pics" a crime. *EuroNews*. https://www.euronews.com/next/2022/03/14/cyberflashing-people-who-send-unwanted-dick-picswill-face-jail-under-uk-s-new-online-safe
Hutt, J. (2019). Offline: Challenging internet and social media bans for individuals on supervision for sex offenses. *NYU Review of Law & Social Change, 43*, 663–705.

Johansen, K. B. H., & Tjørnhøj-Thomsen, T. 'It's like you're almost being exposed to like a flasher'—Unwanted digital sexual attention and gendered vulnerability in a Nordic context (Unpublished manuscript).

Karasavva, V. (2020). *iPredator: Image-based sexual abuse risk factors and motivators* (Doctoral dissertation). Carleton University.

Klettke, B., Hallford, D. J., & Mellor, D. J. (2014). Sexting prevalence and correlates: A systematic literature review. *Clinical Psychology Review, 34*(1), 44–53.

Latimer, B. (2018). Grindr security flaw exposes users' location data. *NBC News*. https://www.nbcnews.com/feature/nbc-out/security-flaws-gay-dating-app-grindr-expose-users-location-data-n858446

Leinung, K. (2019). *The experience of sexual harassment on dating applications* (Doctoral dissertation). Pace University.

Li, D. K. (2020). Utah man confesses to killing woman after Tinder date, police say. *NBC News*. https://www.nbcnews.com/news/us-news/utah-man-confesses-killing-woman-after-tinder-date-police-say-n1214276

Lippman, J. R., & Campbell, S. W. (2014). Damned if you do, damned if you don't ... if you're a girl: Relational and normative contexts of adolescent sexting in the United States. *Journal of Children and Media, 8*(4), 371–386.

Littlewood, A. (2003). Cyberporn and moral panic: An evaluation of press reactions to pornography on the internet. *Library and Information Research, 27*(86), 8–18.

Lopes, M., & Vogel, C. (2017). Women's perspective on using tinder: A user study of gender dynamics in a mobile device application. In *Proceedings of the 35th ACM international conference on the design of communication.*

Lyons, M., Houghton, E., Brewer, G., & O'Brien, F. (2020). The dark triad and sexual assertiveness predict sexual coercion differently in men and women. *Journal of Interpersonal Violence*, advance online copy.

March, E., Grieve, R., Marrington, J., & Jonason, P. K. (2017). Trolling on Tinder® (and other dating apps): Examining the role of the Dark Tetrad and impulsivity. *Personality and Individual Differences, 110*, 139–143.

Marcotte, A. S., Gesselman, A. N., Fisher, H. E., & Garcia, J. R. (2021). Women's and men's reactions to receiving unsolicited genital images from men. *The Journal of Sex Research, 58*(4), 512–521.

Markey, P. M., & Ferguson, C. J. (2017). Teaching us to fear: The violent video game moral panic and the politics of game research. *American Journal of Play, 10*(1), 99–115.

McGlynn, C., Johnson, K., Rackley, E., Henry, N., Gavey, N., Flynn, A., & Powell, A. (2020). 'It's torture for the soul': The harms of image-based sexual abuse. *Social & Legal Studies*, advance online publication.

Melley, B. (2018). Tinder firing back at billboard linking apps to STD spread. *CTV News*. https://www.ctvnews.ca/sci-tech/tinder-firing-back-at-billboards-linking-apps-to-std-spread-1.2585729

Mico, D. J. (2019). Protecting the digital playground: Narrowly tailoring the meaning of social media to prohibit sexual predators from using social media. *McGeorge Law Review, 51*, 123–154.

Moore, A. (2014). How Tinder took me from serial monogamy to casual sex. *The Guardian*. https://www.theguardian.com/lifeandstyle/2014/sep/28/tinder-serial-monogamy-casual-sex

Mori, C., Cooke, J. E., Temple, J. R., Ly, A., Lu, Y., Anderson, N., & Madigan, S. (2020). The prevalence of sexting behaviors among emerging adults: A meta-analysis. *Archives of Sexual Behavior*, 1–17.

Morin, A. (2015). Parents should be concerned about teen use of Tinder. *VeryWellFamily*. https://www.verywellfamily.com/what-every-parent-needs-to-know-about-tinder-2609052

Murphy, A. (2017). Dating dangerously: Risks lurking within mobile dating apps. *Catholic University Journal of Law and Technology, 26*(1), 100–126.

National Crime Agency. (2016). *Emerging new threat in online dating: Initial rends in internet dating-initiated serious sexual assaults*. Author.

NBC. (2022, August 23). California bill allows lawsuits over 'cyber flashing.' *Author*. https://www.nbclosangeles.com/news/california-news/california-cyber-flashing-bill-unsolicited-sexually-graphic-material-gavin-newsom/2969736/

Nguyen, N. (2018). There's a simple fix, but Grindr is still exposing the location of its users. *BuzzFeed News*. https://www.buzzfeednews.com/article/nicolenguyen/grindr-location-data-exposed

North, A. (2019). One state has banned unsolicited dick pics. Will it fix the problem? *Vox*. https://www.vox.com/policy-and-politics/2019/9/3/20847447/unsolicited-dick-pics-texas-law-harassment

Pabian, S., De Backer, C. J., & Vandebosch, H. (2015). Dark Triad personality traits and adolescent cyber-aggression. *Personality and Individual Differences, 75*, 41–46.

Paul, K. (2018). Dating app users take more risks with their sexual health. *New York Post*. https://nypost.com/2018/10/03/dating-app-users-take-more-risks-with-their-sexual-health/

Police Service of Northern Ireland. (n.d.). Sextortion. *Author*. https://www.psni.police.uk/advice_information/sextortion/

Pooley, K., & Boxall, H. (2020). Mobile dating applications and sexual and violent offending. *Trends and Issues in Crime and Criminal Justice, 612*, 1–16.

Powell, A., & Henry, N. (2017). *Sexual violence in a digital age*. Palgrave Macmillan.

Powell, A., Henry, N., & Flynn, A. (2018). Image-based sexual abuse. In W. S. DeKeseredy & M. Dragiewicz (Eds.), *Routledge handbook of critical criminology* (2nd ed., pp. 305–315). Routledge.

Ranzini, G., & Lutz, C. (2017). Love at first swipe? Explaining Tinder self-presentation and motives. *Mobile Media & Communication, 5*(1), 80–101.

Ritzau. (2018). Minister vil sætte en stopper for uønskede 'dick pics' blandt unge. *TV2*. http://nyheder.tv2.dk/politik/2018-09-15-minister-vil-saette-en-stopper-for-uoenskede-dick-pics-blandt-unge.

Rosenfeld, M. J., Thomas, R. J., & Hausen, S. (2019). Disintermediating your friends: How online dating in the United States displaces other ways of meeting. *Proceedings of the National Academy of Sciences, 116*(36), 17753–17758.

Rowse, J., Bolt, C., & Gaya, S. (2020). Swipe right: The emergence of dating-app facilitated sexual assault. A descriptive retrospective audit of forensic examination caseload in an Australian metropolitan service. *Forensic Science, Medicine and Pathology, 16*, 71–77. https://doi.org/10.1007/s12024-019-00201-7

Ruvalcaba, Y., Stephens, D. P., Eaton, A. A., & Boyd, B. (2020). Hispanic women's perceptions of teenage sexting: Qualitative analyses using a sexual scripting framework. *Culture, Health & Sexuality*, 1–16.

Sales, N. J. (2015). Tinder and the dawn of the "dating apocalypse." *Vanity Fair*. https://www.vanityfair.com/culture/2015/08/tinder-hook-up-culture-end-of-dating

Sawyer, A. N., Smith, E. R., & Benotsch, E. G. (2018). Dating application use and sexual risk behavior among young adults. *Sexuality Research and Social Policy, 15*, 183–191.

Scannell, M. J. (2019). Online dating and the risk of sexual assault to college students. *Building Healthy Academic Communities Journal, 3*(1), 34–43.

Schrock, A. R. (2015). Communicative affordances of mobile media: Portability, availability, locatability, and multimediality. *International Journal of Communication, 9*, 1229–1246.

Sevi, B. (2019a). Brief report: Tinder users are risk takers and have low sexual disgust sensitivity. *Evolutionary Psychological Science, 5*(1), 104–108.

Sevi, B. (2019). The dark side of tinder. *Journal of Individual Differences*, advance online copy.

Sevi, B., Aral, T., & Eskenazi, T. (2018). Exploring the hook-up app: Low sexual disgust and high sociosexuality predict motivation to use Tinder for casual sex. *Personality and Individual Differences, 133*, 17–20.

Shapiro, G. K., Tatar, O., Sutton, A., Fisher, W., Naz, A., Perez, S., & Rosberger, Z. (2017). Correlates of Tinder use and risky sexual behaviors in young adults. *Cyberpsychology, Behavior, and Social Networking, 20*(12), 727–734.

Shaw, F. (2016). "Bitch I said hi": The Bye Felipe campaign and discursive activism in mobile dating apps. *Social Media + Society*, *2*(4), 1–10.

Smith, A. (2016a). *15% of American adults have used online dating sites or mobile dating apps*. Pew Research Center.

Smith, A., & Duggan, M. (2013). *Online dating and relationships*. Pew Research Center. https://www.pewresearch.org/internet/2013/10/21/online-dating-relationships/

Smith, C. J. (2016b). *Examining sexual harassment in online dating contexts* (Master's thesis). Illinois State University.

Snaychuk, L. A., & O'Neill, M. L. (2020). Technology-facilitated sexual violence: Prevalence, risk, and resiliency in undergraduate students. *Journal of Aggression, Maltreatment & Trauma, 29*(8), 984–999.

Sokmensuer, H. (2020). Nebraska woman, 24, was lured on Tinder date before couple strangled and dismembered her. *People*. https://people.com/crime/sydney-loofe-lured-tinder-couple-murder/

Stampler, L. (2014). Inside Tinder: Meet the guys who turned dating into an addiction. *Time*. http://time.com/4837/tinder-meet-the-guys-who-turned-dating-into-an-addiction/

Steele, A. R., Hadad, S., Ingham, J. T., Megahey, R. B., Nilan, G. F., Phillpott, J. E., ... & Monson, O. (2025). 'You don't look for love on grindr, that's for sure': A qualitative investigation into dating app use of Australian same-sex attracted men. *Psychology & Sexuality, 16*(1), 232–246.

Steinbuch, Y. (2020). New Zealand man who killed backpacker Grace Millane had attacked other women. *New York Post*. https://nypost.com/2020/12/23/man-who-killed-backpacker-grace-millane-had-attacked-other-women/

Stiff, C. (2019). The dark triad and Facebook surveillance: How Machiavellianism, psychopathy, but not narcissism predict using Facebook to spy on others. *Computers in Human Behavior, 94*, 62–69.

Suler, J. (2004). The online disinhibition effect. *Cyberpsychology & Behavior, 7*(3), 321–326.

Sumter, S. R., Vandenbosch, L., & Ligtenberg, L. (2017). Love me Tinder: Untangling emerging adults' motivations for using the dating application Tinder. *Telematics and Informatics, 34*(1), 67–78.

Thiel-Stern, S. (2014). *From the dance hall to Facebook: Teen girls, mass media, and moral panic in the United States, 1905–2010*. University of Massachusetts Press.

Thompson, L. (2018). "I can be your Tinder nightmare": Harassment and misogyny in the online sexual marketplace. *Feminism & Psychology, 28*(1), 69–89.

Timmermans, E., & De Caluwé, E. (2017). Development and validation of the Tinder Motives Scale (TMS). *Computers in Human Behavior, 70*, 341–350.

Tinder. (2021). Tinder. https://tinder.com/en

Tomaszewska, P., & Schuster, I. (2020). Comparing sexuality-related cognitions, sexual behavior, and acceptance of sexual coercion in dating app users and non-users. *Sexuality Research and Social Policy, 17*(2), 188–198.

Tsekouras, P. (2021). Multipl reports of dating app 'sextortion' scams in York Region, police issue warning. *CTV News*. https://toronto.ctvnews.ca/multiple-reports-of-dating-app-sextortion-scams-in-york-region-police-issue-warning-1.5316011

Tweten, A. (2014). Why I created Bye Felipe. *Ms. Magazine*. http://msmagazine.com/blog/2014/10/31/why-i-created-bye-felipe/

van Geel, M., Goemans, A., Toprak, F., & Vedder, P. (2017). Which personality traits are related to traditional bullying and cyberbullying? A study with the Big Five, Dark Triad and sadism. *Personality and Individual Differences, 106*, 231–235.

Vitis, L., & Gilmour, F. (2017). Dick pics on blast: A woman's resistance to online sexual harassment using humour, art and Instagram. *Crime, Media, Culture, 13*(3), 335–355.

Waling, A., & Pym, T. (2017). 'C'mon, no one wants a dick pic': Exploring the cultural framings of the 'Dick Pic' in contemporary online publics. *Journal of Gender Studies, 28*(1), 70–85.

Wang, H., Zhang, L., Zhou, Y., Wang, K., Zhang, X., Wu, J., & Wang, G. (2018). The use of geosocial networking smartphone applications and the risk of sexually transmitted infections among men who have sex with men: A systematic review and meta-analysis. *BMC Public Health, 18*(1), 1–10.

Brandon Sparks, PhD, FHEA is a Postdoctoral Fellow at the University of New Brunswick investigation police responses to intimate partner violence cases. He received his MA and PhD from the University of Saskatchewan. His research interests span the nexus between healthy and unhealthy relationships with an emphasis on sexual violence, particularly technology-facilitated sexual violence. He has also published research exploring the psychosocial issues experienced by members of the involuntary celibacy (incel) community.

CHAPTER 6

Incels (Involuntary Celibates): Diagnosing the Effects of the Black Pill

William Costello

Some guys have all the luck.
Some guys have all the pain.
Some guys get all the breaks.
Some guys do nothing but complain.
Rod Stewart

Incels

Involuntary celibates (incels) are a primarily online sub-culture community of men who forge a sense of identity around their perceived inability to form sexual or romantic relationships. The incel community operates almost exclusively online, providing an outlet to express misogynistic hostility, frustration, and blame toward society for a perceived failure to

W. Costello (✉)
University of Texas at Austin, Austin, TX, USA
e-mail: williamcostello@utexas.edu

C. A. Harper et al. (eds.), *Sexual Crime and the Internet*, Sexual Crime,
https://doi.org/10.1007/978-3-031-95844-1_6

include them (Speckhard et al., 2021). In recent years, the online community of incels has risen to the top of the security policy agenda. This is, in large part, due to several high-profile attacks resulting in 59 deaths (Hoffman et al., 2020). This chapter reviews and synthesizes the current literature on incels, outlining the historical development of the community, their demographic profile, ideological worldview, and potentiality for harm to themselves and others.

History of the Incel Community

The term "involuntary celibate" was coined in 1997 by a Canadian woman who wanted to create a space for men and women who were struggling to find romance (Andersen, 2023). The first incel subreddit "r/ForeverAlone" was created in 2010, but the movement started to gain traction in the latter half of that decade, after another subreddit "r/Incels" appeared, until its ban in 2017. Afterwards the movement grew outwards, both to other subreddits (e.g., "r/braincels") or to forums on other parts of the web, such as "incels.is" (Ribeiro et al., 2021). Given the cross-platform nature of the movement and the fact that many platforms are anonymous in nature, it is difficult to ascertain exactly how many incels there are. However, "r/Incels" had 40,000 users in 2016 (Hoffman et al., 2020), although on a popular forum such as Reddit, it is unlikely that all users were incels. The forum "incels.is" currently has over 20,000 registered users, so it is likely that the movement counts its followers in the tens of thousands.

There is some debate about the definition of, and criteria for, inceldom. Indeed, Speckhard et al. (2021) found that when offered a list of potential requirements, incels themselves were not in agreement regarding what constitutes inceldom. The popular incel site, "Incels.Wiki" (2021) suggests the following definition of inceldom:

> *…a gender-neutral life circumstance…Incels are highly diverse politically, racially, religiously, and socioeconomically…Different incels have different views on the causes of involuntary celibacy and possible solutions to alleviate this circumstance…No philosophy represents all incels.*

While Donnelly et al. (2001) define incels as "all adults who fail to find a sexual partner for six months or more, despite their desire to do so", Costello et al. (2023) suggest that any definition based on a metric of time is too broad and does not reflect the incel social identity or worldview. Due to the subjective nature of involuntary celibacy (i.e., it is impossible to prove that an individual objectively cannot form sexual or romantic relationships), the identity requires an individual to embrace it and integrate it into their sense of self (Costello, 2023; Rousis et al., 2023). Ellenberg et al. (2023) conducted a cluster analysis of incels to demarcate three different ideological narratives that exist among incels: *Externalizers* who blame society, *hopers* seeking improvement, and *internalizers* who blame themselves and experience intense emotional distress.

Incel Ideology/Worldview

Given the large number of incels online today and a limited empirical research base, it is difficult to ascribe a "core ideology" that is shared by all members of the movement (Hart & Huber, 2023). However, there are some broadly shared beliefs that tie the movement together. Incels purport that genetic factors evolved mate preferences, and inequitable social structures restrict their access to sexual relationships with women (Brooks et al., 2022). They believe that most women are attracted to a small number of men (who they refer to as *Chads*), who monopolize sexual encounters, while the "*genetically inferior*" incels are excluded from the gene pool (Baselice, 2023; Blake & Brooks, 2022). In this sense, incels differ from many existing extremist groups. Rather than striving to change society, incels are more focused on justifying what they perceive to be their hopeless existence (Cottee, 2020).

There is some evidence that incels are *partially accurate* about the socioeconomic factors contributing to their plight. Incel activity is sensitive to the local mating ecology (Brooks et al., 2022), i.e., incels are more prevalent in geographic areas of: *high income-inequality* (fewer high-status men for women to compete for), *low gender pay gaps* (where women do not need to settle for men out of economic necessity) and *male-biased sex ratios* (fewer single women).

Incels often claim the dating market is biased against unattractive men. They believe that 80% of the women are only sexually interested in the top 20% of men, leaving the bottom 80% of men with the attention of just 20% of women (Costello et al., 2025). When asked about the 80/20 rule, almost two thirds of incels ($n = 374$) indicated that they personally agreed with it, while more than 80% ($n = 448$) felt that most incels agreed with it (Costello et al., 2023).

Although the incel worldview is an extreme, hyperbolic caricature of the attraction inequality of the mating market, there is some evidence supporting the notion that a small group of men have a higher number of sexual partners compared to the majority. For instance: a study by Harper et al. (2017) revealed that while the average number of partners men had remained consistent between 2002 and 2013, the top 20% of men experienced a 25% surge in the number of sexual partners. Even more striking, the top 5% of men witnessed a 38% increase. Similarly, Räsänen (2023) reported an upward trend in the number of young men not having any sexual encounters. At the same time, there's a subset of men reporting an increased number of sexual partners. To provide specific numbers: in 2002, the most active 20% of American heterosexual men reported 12 lifetime partners, while the top 5% reported 38 partners. By 2012, these numbers rose to 15 partners for the top 20% and 50 partners for the top 5%. The overall median number of partners remained unchanged. Interestingly, there was no corresponding increase observed among heterosexual women. These findings suggest that sexual activity is not spread evenly across the male population but seems concentrated within a specific group of men who are very active.

According to Baele and colleagues (2021, 2023), incel ideology categorizes people into one of three categories of physical attractiveness: The hyper-attractive Chads and Stacys who have their pick of the sexual marketplace, followed by average-looking "betas" (or "normies"), and then at the bottom of the pile, physically unattractive men who cannot find a mate (incels). Given this hierarchy, many incels subscribe to a worldview known as the "black pill". The black pill is a derivative of the concept of taking the red pill, from the movie The Matrix, which denotes a willingness to "see the world as it really is", as opposed to the "blissful ignorance" of taking the blue pill (Wachowski et al., 1999). The black pill describes a particularly bleak "truth" to swallow; the belief that sexual attraction is mostly fixed and there is nothing that incels can do to improve their romantic prospects (Glace et al., 2021). It is worth noting that ~95% of incels report to subscribe to the worldview known as the black pill (Speckhard et al., 2021).

Incel Demographics

Many commentators describe the incelosphere (incel community) as adjacent to far-right or white-supremacist movements (Bates, 2020; Srinivasan, 2021). However, Costello et al. (2022) found ethnic diversity within the incelosphere, with 36% identifying as BIPOC (black, indigenous, person of colour). The largest study of incels to date (n = 561) Costello et al. (2023) found that 42% of their exclusively US or UK sample of incels identified as BIPOC (Black Indigenous or Person of Colour).

In terms of politics, Costello et al. (2022) found that 39% of incels reported to be right leaning, 45% identified as left leaning, and 17% said they were centrist. When asked about their political orientation via a series of binary policy position questions (derived from the Pew Research Ideological Consistency Scale), incels were slightly left of centre. The only "right-wing" views that were selected by the majority of incels were that the "Government is almost always wasteful and inefficient" and feeling that "Ethnic minorities who can't get ahead in this country are mostly responsible for their own condition". On the other hand, they were substantially left of centre on questions regarding homosexuality, corporate profits, and social benefits (Costello et al., 2023).

Separately, Jaki et al. (2019) used a dictionary-based approach to identify posts on the incel forum "Incels.is" with keywords that constitute racism, finding that just 3% could be considered racist. Although extreme racialized derogatory slang can be seen throughout the incelosphere, Pelzer et al. (2021) found that "self-hatred" is a significantly more common form of "toxic language" in the forum "Incels.co.", concluding that the racism on incel forums is not comparable to white-supremacist forums. Finally, Costello et al. (2022) found that incels were highly likely to be NEET (Not in Education Employment or Training) and still living with their parents into adulthood.

The Tendency for Interpersonal Victimhood

Costello et al. (2022) found that incels have a significant *tendency for interpersonal victimhood* (TIV). The TIV describes an ongoing feeling that the self is a victim, which becomes central to one's identity (Gabay et al., 2020). The TIV is comprised of four dimensions: *Need for recognition*: the preoccupation with having the legitimacy of grievances acknowledged, ***moral elitism***: the belief that the individual or their ingroup behaves more morally than others, ***lack of empathy***: the belief that because of their victimization, an individual cares less about the pain of others, and ***rumination***: the preoccupation with reflecting on past instances of victimization. Those with a perpetual victimhood mindset tend to have an external locus of control regarding their life. Incels take an external locus of control to the extreme (Brzuskiewicz, 2020). Indicative of this mindset is the fact that Approximately 95% of incels subscribe to the worldview known as the black pill (Speckhard et al., 2021). This belief in the permanency of inceldom predicted high levels of depression (Costello et al., 2022). Conventional strategies of persuasion tend to be ineffective against people (such as incels) who are highly *certain* of their beliefs (Swann et al., 1988). *Cracking* the certainty of incels' belief in the black pill presents a formidable challenge in directing incels toward less problematic identities.

The Self-Verification of Incel Identity vs. Participation in an Anxiety-Inducing Mating Market

The *need to belong* theory suggests that humans have a fundamental motivation to be a part of social groups (Baumeister & Leary, 1995). It is possible that incels experience many positives from the social-identity of inceldom, when compared with participating in what they see as an anxiety-inducing mating market (Zdjelar, 2020).

In line with the *need for recognition* dimension of the tendency for interpersonal victimhood, incels appear to prefer having their self-view verified by other incels (Rousis et al., 2023). Incel identity also provides a sense of fraternity (Crimando, 2019), a virtuous victimhood identity (Ok et al., 2021), a common enemy (Lindsay, 2022), and a rich lexicon of in-group terminology (Gothard, 2020). As such, it may be preferable for many incels to reinforce their incel identity than to participate in an anxiety inducing mating market (Costello et al., 2023).

Furthermore, Hinds (2022) and Costello (2023) outline that members of online incel forums often limit other members from engaging with the mating market, even banning them from forums if they report any semblance of romantic success. Costello et al. (2023) suggest that future research should ascertain how participation in the mating market affects incels, and for which individuals' incel identity provides comfort rather than feelings of hopelessness.

Why Worry About Incels?

Although it is unclear how much of incel rhetoric is performatively antagonistic, online misogyny can be used to predict instances of domestic violence (Blake et al., 2021). There is also evidence that internet "trolls" who are hostile online are similarly hostile offline (Bor & Peterson, 2022), and they may be attracted to evolutionarily novel online worlds where they can pursue aggression-based strategies without risking real-world retaliation. Blake and Brooks (2022) make a compelling case for why society should not ignore its incel problem, outlining that there is robust evidence for what is referred to in the evolutionary psychology literature as the *Young Male Syndrome* (Wilson & Daly, 1985). The Young Male Syndrome refers to the tendency for surplus populations of unpartnered young men to disproportionately harm society and themselves, due to increased status seeking and risk taking in pursuit of mates (Edlund et al., 2013; Guttentag & Secord, 1983; Krahn et al., 1986). There is also accumulating evidence from criminology for the sexual frustration theory of aggression, violence, and crime (Lankford, 2021). Research also shows that unwanted celibacy is associated with misogynistic attitudes among men (Granau et al., 2022). These lines of evidence should give us cause for concern about the problems incels face and represent in society and highlight the importance of planning appropriate interventions.

High-Profile Instances of Incel Violence

Incel stories garner significant media attention, often fixating on misogyny and violence. Elliot Rodger is the most infamous incel killer. In 2014, he killed six people and injured fourteen others—by gunshot, stabbing, and vehicle ramming—near the University of California, Isla Vista, Santa Barbara campus before killing himself. Rodger emailed his 107,000-word manifesto (Rodger, 2014), *My Twisted World: The Story of Elliot Rodger*, to 34 people, including his therapist, his parents, and other family, former teachers, and childhood friends. In his last YouTube video, "*Elliot Rodger's Retribution*", Rodger complained of being rejected by women and envying sexually active men and described his planned attack and the motives behind it. In the video, he says:

> *Tomorrow is the day of retribution, the day in which I will have my revenge against humanity, against all of you. For the last eight years of my life,*

ever since I hit puberty, I've been forced to endure an existence of loneliness, rejection, and unfulfilled desires all because girls have never been attracted to me. Girls gave their affection, and sex, and love to other men but never to me. I'm 22 years old and I'm still a virgin. I've never even kissed a girl. I've been through college for two and a half years, more than that actually, and I'm still a virgin. It has been very torturous. College is the time when everyone experiences those things such as sex and fun and pleasure. Within those years, I've had to rot in loneliness. It's not fair. You girls have never been attracted to me. I don't know why you girls aren't attracted to me, but I will punish you all for it. It's an injustice, a crime, because ... I don't know what you don't see in me. I'm the perfect guy and yet you throw yourselves at these obnoxious men instead of me, the supreme gentleman.

In Canada, there is the case of Alek Minassian. Ten of the 59 deaths attributable to incel violence can be accounted for by Alek Minassian alone, who in 2018 used a rental van to kill ten people in Toronto. Minassian's case is attractive to the media because of a Facebook post he made the night before his actions, saying that "The Incel Rebellion has already begun! We will overthrow the Chads and Stacys! All hail the Supreme Gentleman Elliot Rodger".

Elliot Rodger and Alek Minassian are often presented as the "poster boys" of the incel community. However, the grandiose narcissism of Elliot Rodger may not be common among incels. Indeed, incels typically suffer from low self-esteem (Costello et al., 2022; Sparks et al., 2022). Also, less frequently reported in the media is the following element of the judge's verdict on Alek Minassian's case (Minassian, 2021), where he was sentenced to life in prison with no possibility of parole for 25 years:

He told lies deliberately to depict the killings as being connected to the incel movement & get more media attention...He piggybacked on the incel movement to ratchet up his own notoriety. His story to the police about the attack being an "incel rebellion" was a lie.

There is also the tragic case of Jake Davison, who, in the first alleged incel attack in the UK in 2021, used a pump action shotgun to kill five people, including his mother and a 3-year-old girl, and injure two others before killing himself. Davison's social media contributions very closely align with the stereotypical incel prose and concerns, tapping into typical ideas such as men being oppressed through women denying them sex (Brace et al., 2023). However, again less frequently reported is the fact that Deputy senior national coordinator for UK counterterrorism policing, Tim Jacques, concluded that Jake Davison was "not motivated by the misogynistic incel online movement, and the shooting was not terror-related and the incel ideology is not a terrorist movement" (Hamilton, 2021).

One fundamental problem with the typical media misrepresentation of incels is that they frequently go against the guidelines of the *Institute for Research on Male Supremacism*, which suggest that we should incorporate a "no notoriety" protocol when reporting on incel violence (IRSM, n.d.).

Should Incels Be Classified as a Terrorist Group?

There is some debate as to whether incels should be considered a terrorist movement. In his review of the UK's Counterterrorism Prevent Strategy, William Shawcross (2023) notes that he agrees with the deputy senior national co-ordinator for counterterrorism, who argues that they should *not* be considered as such because they do not fit the criteria of using violence to further ideology. On the other hand, Hoffman et al. (2020) argue that proponents of incel-related violence have become emboldened online and "there is ample reason to believe violent incels remain a grave terrorism threat". Looking at the most recent Prevent figures, incels make up a relatively small proportion of the number of referrals (77 in total, or 1.2% of all referrals). However, incel-related cases were most likely to be adopted by a Channel panel as a case (23 out of 23, or 68%) of any recognized movement (Home Office, 2023). This suggests that while the number of cases is small in number, those that are referred may pose some kind of violent threat. The number of terrorist plots that can be described as "incel" is contested, the Anti-Defamation League lists 31 attacks under their "Incel Backgrounder", although this includes individuals such as the Plymouth attacker in 2021, whose plot the UK Government have declined to label terrorism (Hall, 2023) and an individual who committed his attack in 1989, long before the present incel community existed. Hoffman et al. (2020) develop a more nuanced four-tier typography of "Clear Incel Attacks", "Attacks with Mixed-Motives that Evidence Incel Ideology", "Acts of Targeted Violence by Incels", and "Ex-Post Facto Inceldom" which provide a more rigorous understanding of incel terrorism. However, Cottee (2020), suggests it would be a mistake to categorize incel violence as terrorism, since the community does not advocate the use of violence as a necessary remedy for in-group defence.

Regardless of whether the community is a *terrorist* threat or not, there is consensus that it meets the criteria of hateful extremism; the Commission for Countering Extremism (2021) notes that the incel subculture meets their own definition. Similarly, in the Prevent review, Shawcross (2023) argues that the community should be countered under hate crime legislation, while the Law Commission (2021) extended existing legislation to protect women and girls, which they explicitly link to the "growing threat from incels calling for the rape and/or murder of women". Analyses of the incel ecosystem have repeatedly demonstrated high levels of toxic and misogynistic language. Baele et al. (2023) find that discussions within the "incelosphere" have steadily become more violent and extreme in recent years. Similarly, Ribeiro et al. (2021) who conducted an ecosystem analysis of the entire manosphere, found that newer groups such as Men Going Their Own Way and incels had grown in popularity at the expense of older ones (e.g., Men's Rights Activists and Pick Up Artists). Importantly, they find that the newer communities are more toxic and misogynistic than their forerunners.

Incel Violence in Perspective

Many authors draw allusions to incel ideology and violent extremism. The empirical evidence for such a link is less clear. Firstly, we must put the extent of incel violence into context and compare it to other terrorist groups, as it has been suggested that incels should be categorized as a terrorist group (Hoffman et al., 2020). Reports now number incel membership in the United States from around 40,000 (Beauchamp, 2019) to hundreds of thousands (Kutchinsky, 2019), and at the time of writing there are approximately 20,000 active users of the main forum Incels.co. It is estimated that incels have killed approximately 59 people worldwide (Hoffman et al., 2020). In contrast, the similarly sized (approximately 15,000 members) Islamist terrorist group Boko Haram, has killed an estimated 350,000 people since 2002 (Reuters, 2023).

One of the largest incel studies ($n = 274$) found that incel ideology was only weakly correlated with radicalization, and most incels in the study ($n = 219$, 80%) rejected violence. Moskalenko et al. (2022) asked incels (scored on a five-point scale, with 1 = "not at all", and 5 = "very much") about attitudes toward Incel violence. The average incel score for the specific item "I admire Elliot Rodger for his Santa Barbara attack", was (M = 1.83; SD = 1.25). Another report from the International Centre for Counterterrorism used LIWC (Linguistic Inquiry and Word Count) software to analyze language (Pennebaker et al., 2001) in incel, MGTOW (Men Going Their Own Way), pick up artist, and right-wing forums. Just 1.39% of incel posts could be categorized as legitimizing violence, the second lowest of the groups (Perliger et al., 2023).

Costello et al. (2023) surveyed 561 rigorously screened incels from the United States and the United Kingdom. When asked if they would ever justify violence against people that incels perceive as causing harm to them, around one quarter incels (n = 140) picked either "Sometimes" or "Often", while those who picked "Often" formed just over 5% (n = 28). Although this means that the average response sat between "Never" and "Rarely", these are still alarmingly high response rates for this measure, supporting some research which finds that violence is regularly supported within incel communities (Baele et al., 2021). This is also somewhat in line with other incel-related research; Speckhard et al. (2021) asked participants whether they sometimes entertain thoughts of violence toward others, of which 26% responded affirmatively. At the same time, this level of approval of violence seems normal compared to recent nationally representative research, such as that by Wintemute et al. (2022), who found that 20% of the United States public thought that violence is sometimes, usually, or always justified.

Overall, there does not seem to be compelling evidence, despite a small number of highly florid cases that received tremendous news attention, that incels are particularly prone to real-world violence.

What About Sexual Violence?

Sparks and colleagues (2022, 2023) suggest that the term incel has resulted in an overemphasis on the sexual frustration aspects of incel identity. This overemphasis has led many to speculate about the sexual violence threat presented by incels. However, even in the high-profile cases of incel violence, there has been a conspicuous absence of sexual violence. This is in line with the lack of support in the literature for the *mate deprivation hypothesis of rape*. Most men who commit acts of sexual violence are men who are already sexually successful (Buss, 2021).

A common measure used to ascertain men's propensity for sexual violence is to ask about their *willingness to rape if you could get away with it*. Perhaps counterintuitively, incels score significantly lower than the general population in this measure. Speckhard et al. (2021) found that 13.6% of incels reported *some* willingness to rape if they could get away with it. Conversely, ~35%, ~20–25%, ~19%, and ~30% of men in the general population, respectively, reported *some* willingness to rape if they could get away with it (Hahnel-Peeters et al., 2022; Malamuth, 1981; Palmer et al., 2021; Young & Thiessen, 1992). This is despite incels scoring higher in measures of Hostile Sexism (Glick & Fiske, 2018) and Rape Myth Acceptance (Bendixen & Kennair, 2017), than general population estimates (Costello et al., 2023).

In sum, even when it comes to sexual violence specifically, incels do not appear to be more likely, and in fact may be less likely, to commit it.

A More Puzzling Question: Why Aren't Incels More Violent?

Given our understanding of the Young Male Syndrome, the perplexing question is why there hasn't been a surge in violence accompanying the rising rates of sexlessness (Pinker, 2018; Räsänen, 2023). Fleischman (2020) posits that contemporary men might find their ambition for status diverted and diminished by immersive online activities like video games and pornography. Pornography might offer deceptive signals to men, making them feel their sexual desires are being fulfilled, especially when compared to the often anxiety-ridden and competitive real-world mating arena. Cues from the environment that imply there's no need for risky behaviours to achieve reproductive success can diminish the drive for such actions. This could be one explanation for the observed decrease in sexual assault rates associated with the increasing prevalence of pornography (Diamond, 1999; Diamond et al., 2011; Kutchinsky, 1973, 1991). Costello and Buss (2023) offer one speculative hypothesis as to why there does not appear to be a corresponding spike in violence, both sexual and non-sexual, alongside increasing rates of sexlessness. The *Male Sedation Hypothesis* calls for future work to empirically test the Male Sedation Hypothesis, i.e., whether online worlds have a pacifying effect on the potentiality for violence among sexless young men.

Extreme Inceldom and Suicidality

A comprehensive literature review found that while mental-health issues are prominent points of discussion on incel forums, they have not received the same attention as themes of misogyny (Stijelja & Mishara, 2022). This is despite romantic relationships being a robust predictor of mental well-being (Pietromonaco & Beck, 2019; Raque-Bogdan et al., 2011), and negative relations between depressive symptoms and assessment of one's own mate value (Kirsner et al., 2003). From an evolutionary perspective, failure to satisfy such fundamental needs as mating and pair-bonding can be expected to have deleterious consequences for well-being, mental health, and social functioning (Baumeister & Leary, 1995; Kenrick et al., 2010). Indeed, Apostolou et al. (2019) found that people who indicated *poor mating performance* experienced more negative emotions such as sadness and loneliness, and fewer positive emotions such as happiness and excitement, and lower life satisfaction. Van De Velde et al. (2010) found that *being single* was a large risk factor for high levels of depression in men, and Brody (2010) found that psychological function was positively correlated (sometimes showing a causational relationship) with penile-vaginal intercourse.

Several studies find extremely poor mental health among incels (Moskalenko et al., 2022; Speckhard & Ellenberg, 2022). Using clinical measures, Costello et al. (2022) found that 73% of incels were severely or moderately depressed, and 67% were severely or moderately anxious. These data are concerning given the relationship between suicide risk and depression and anxiety in men (Bjerkeset et al., 2008). Indeed, many incels openly discuss suicidal plans online (Daly & Laskovtsov, 2021), and 82.3% report to have strongly considered suicide (Incels.co, 2020). When we think about incels in terms of extremism, the evidence suggests that *extreme* inceldom looks more like suicidality than violence toward others. The two strongest correlates of male suicidal ideation are failure in heterosexual mating and burdensomeness to kin (de Catanzaro, 1995). Both factors are extremely salient for incels, many of whom report to be NEET (not in education, employment, or training) and still living with their parents into adulthood (Costello et al., 2022). Indeed, in the largest study of incels to date ($n = 561$), Whittaker et al. (2023) found that a fifth of the sample ($n = 112$) reported experiencing suicidal thoughts *nearly every day* for the past 2 weeks.

Incel suicidality could be framed as *coalitional bargaining for better social treatment*. Hagen (2003) proposes the bargaining model for depression, suggesting that the syndrome functions somewhat like a labour strike, providing evidence that depression is associated with the receipt of considerable social benefits despite the negative reaction it causes in others. The suicidality that pervades the incelosphere could be a response to the perceived ostracism from society (Daly & Nichols, 2023; Daly & Reed, 2022) and an attempt at bargaining for better social treatment.

Additionally, Sparks et al. (2022) highlight how only one-third of "incels.co" users indicated that they had *any* friends. Costello et al. (2022) also found high levels of loneliness among incels, suggesting that they may be missing a key buffer in sheltering them from the adverse effects of romantic rejection. These data are concerning given that meta-analyses show social isolation is associated with increased risk for early mortality (Holt-Lunstad et al., 2015). From an evolutionary psychological perspective, loneliness represents an alarm signal that something is drastically wrong because, in the vast majority of ancestral environments, social isolation would equate to a death sentence. Although this may not be the case in the modern environment per se, our evolved psychological mechanisms are more attuned to the ancestral environments in response to which they evolved (Tooby & Cosmides, 1990). As such, humans process loneliness as catastrophic. It makes sense that loneliness would correlate with broader mental health issues (e.g., depression and anxiety), acting as a cue for incels to engage in bargaining for better treatment.

Autistic Spectrum Disorder Among Incels

One component of incels' psychology that should not be overlooked is the high rates of autism spectrum disorder (ASD) within the community. Speckhard and Ellenberg (2022) found that 18.38% of incels reported having such a diagnosis, with 44% reporting the presence of symptoms of ASD. Troublingly, self-reported intensity of autism spectrum traits was significantly associated with agreement that networking in incel forums made the respondent feel violent (Speckhard & Ellenberg, 2022). Costello et al. (2023) found that approximately 30% of incels pass the cut-off for referral using the AQ-10—a brief questionnaire that primary care practitioners use when deciding to make a referral for an autism spectrum disorder assessment. There is some troubling evidence that ASD may influence, but does not *cause*, individuals to commit extreme violent acts such as mass shootings. Analysis from Allely et al. (2017) provides a conservative estimate of ASD in 6 of 75 mass shooting cases (8%), approximately eight times higher than the prevalence of ASD in the general population (Elsabbagh et al., 2012).

The Effect of Incel Forums

Identity fusion, i.e., a visceral sense of oneness with a group, has been found to predict extreme beliefs/behaviours, e.g., extreme attitudes in gaming (Kowert et al., 2022). Rousis et al. (2023) found that incels display higher levels of identity fusion than other groups, and this predicted endorsement of violence and online harassment toward women. This is unsurprising given that Jaki et al. (2019) found that ~30% of incel posts could be considered misogynistic. Sunstein (1999) has observed that a group often becomes collectively more radical than any of its members when they first joined, and there is some evidence that this is the case with incels (Kiss, 2022). However, Halpin et al. (2023) analysed every comment ($N = 3{,}686{,}110$) produced over 42 months on a popular incel discussion board and found that nearly *all* active participants use misogynistic terms. They found that participants used misogynistic terms nearly one million times and at a rate 2.4 times greater than their use of neutral terms for women. Although the majority of participants' use of misogynistic terms does not increase or decrease with post frequency, suggesting that members arrive (rather than become) misogynistic. Additionally, Costello et al. (2022) showed that forum-using incels reported lower levels of well-being than those who reported not using forums.

Separately, Speckhard et al. (2021) revealed that roughly three quarters of incels reported that forums made them "feel understood", provided "a sense of belonging" or made them "feel less lonely", but a little over half reported that forums made them "feel hopeless".

In the largest study of incels to date, Costello et al. (2023) created a "*Harm*" factor consisting of *angry rumination, revenge planning, displaced aggression, hostile sexism, rape myth acceptance,* and *justification of violence.* They then created three factors to use in combination to predict *Harm.* A *mental health* factor was made from the *loneliness, anxiety, depression, ASD,* and *rejection sensitivity* variables. Next, they formed a *Narrative* factor from feelings of discrimination, shared incel worldview, agreement with the 20/80 concept, and seeing feminists, women, the political left, and wider society as enemies. Finally, they formed a *Network* factor (*number of social networks used, time spent on them, amount of interaction with others, content generation,* and *exposure to radical people and content*). A pathway analysis using Mental Health, Ideology, and Social Networking revealed that all three factors predicted Harm directly. However, the predictive power of Mental Health and Ideology was more than twice that of Networking.

Costello et al. (2023) describe how the dynamic interplay between Mental health, Networking, and Ideology offers a complex yet illuminating lens through which to understand the incel community. Ideology serves as the glue that binds the incel community together. However, as a predominantly online movement, it necessitates and intensifies the need for Networking, with members seeking solace and understanding from like-minded individuals. This increased online interaction in turn has the potential to both amplify and normalize extreme ideological views, which can further exacerbate feelings of alienation, anger, or desolation (Kiss, 2022; Ribeiro et al., 2021). These heightened emotional states may contribute to a deterioration in Mental health, which in turn may contribute to harmful attitudes.

Pre-existing poor mental health can make individuals more susceptible to extreme ideologies, as they may be searching for explanations for their feelings of rejection, loneliness, or despair. The ideological narrative of the incel community, which offers a black and white victimhood rubric through which to view the world, provides an appealing and simplified explanation. This narrative can verify incels' experiences and emotions, leading them to dive deeper into Networking to further engage with these ideologies (Costello, 2023; Kiss, 2022; Rousis et al., 2023).

Additionally, individuals with poor levels of mental health might turn to online Networking as a refuge, given the anonymity and lack of face-to-face interaction it offers. Within these online spaces, they become increasingly exposed to the incel Ideology, which can further entrench their beliefs and attitudes (Ribeiro et al., 2021).

In sum, while each of these factors—Mental health, Networking, and Ideology—have individual implications for incel harm, their combined interaction creates a feedback loop that can intensify harmful beliefs, behaviours, and emotions. Understanding these intricate interactions is crucial for devising effective interventions and support mechanisms for those entrenched in or vulnerable to the incel community.

Incels' Mating Intelligence and Dating Anxiety

Mating intelligence can be described as a constellation of mental adaptations that generate adaptive strategies in human mating, one component of which is cross-sex mindreading, which includes the ability to accurately ascertain what traits members of the opposite sex value in a potential mate (Geher et al., 2016). Costello et al. (2023) found that incels err in this area, i.e., they overestimate the importance of physical attractiveness and financial resources and underestimate women's preferences for kindness, intelligence, and humour. Interventions should help incels to overcome their belief in *female sexual deceptiveness* (Sparks et al., 2022) and acknowledge the importance of these traits to help improve their mating prospects.

Costello et al. (2023) suggest that the failures of cross-sex mind reading found within incels may be an artefact of the high levels of autism spectrum disorder (ASD) that exist within the incel community (Costello et al., 2023; Speckhard et al., 2021), as many people with ASD have a poorer theory of mind, i.e., poorer ability to infer the desires of others (Baron-Cohen, 1990). Płatos et al. (2023) provide some experimental evidence for fostering dating skills among adults with ASD, using interventions based on direct instruction, modelling, and practising social skills in a group setting. Such interventions may be suitable for incels with ASD.

Kugeares (2002) found experimental evidence for an evolved mating-specific anxiety mechanism, the putative function for which is to help solve the adaptive problem of the costliness of being rejected by a potential mate. Ancestral humans residing in small groups with limited geographic mobility would have encountered perhaps a few dozen potential mates in their lifetime (Goetz et al., 2019), and consistent sexual rejection would likely have been perceived as catastrophic. Meanwhile, the modern mating environment, with dating apps, densely populated cities, and easier transportation to meet people beyond our immediate environment, now provide the opportunity for someone to receive more rejections in one day than would have been possible in a lifetime in our ancestral environment. This could amplify any negative effects of rejection on mental health and self-perceived mate value. Excessive swiping on dating apps increased fear of being single and decreased participants' self-esteem (Thomas et al., 2022). Relatedly, incels endorsed "being too anxious around potential partners" as one of the most popular reasons for being single (Costello et al., 2022). Incels may experience *dating anxiety* that would have been functional in our ancestral environment, but maladaptive in our current environment. This is an example of evolutionary mismatch in mating (Goetz et al., 2019). That is, our psychological mechanisms evolved in response to ancestral environments that are meaningfully different than the current environment (Tooby & Cosmides, 1990).

Alongside the aforementioned dating anxiety, Costello et al. (2023) found that incels endorsed "lack of flirting skills" as a common reason for their singlehood. Coupled with incels' cognitive distortions around female mate preferences, this suggests that interventions to improve incel mating intelligence could have efficacy. Research has also shown that male mate value is dependent on much more malleable traits such as status and financial resources, than female mate value, which is more contingent on physical attractiveness and youth (Ben-Hamida et al., 1998). As such, incels mate value could potentially be improved upon. There is some evidence that interventions designed to improve social confidence had real impacts on men's prospects in speed-dating scenarios (Li et al., 2020). Such interventions could be appropriate for incels.

Correcting cognitive distortions (Gilbert, 1998) around female mate preferences could be an avenue of exploration to improve incels' mating performance and any subsequent mental health issues (Apostolou et al., 2019, 2023). Research shows that unwanted celibacy is associated with misogynistic attitudes among men (Granau et al., 2022). Thus, designing interventions to help incels achieve their mating goals could have the potential added benefit of reducing harmful instances of misogyny. Incel misogyny likely has a bidirectional relationship with their mating prospects. Interventions that prioritize reducing incel misogyny prior to, or alongside, improving their mating intelligence, could have more efficacy. Importantly, such interventions might also reduce the potentiality for harm toward women.

Sexual Entitlement?

Another significant narrative in the mainstream media suggests that incels feel aggrieved that their sense-of-entitlement to attractive women is thwarted (Srinivasan, 2021). However, there are some data to challenge the pervasive view of incels as *entitled*. For instance, incels report significantly *lower* standards for minimum mate preferences than non-incel single men, and report more liberal dating app strategies such as swiping right on a wider range of profiles (Costello et al., 2023; Sparks et al., 2023). This suggests that incels do not feel entitled to disproportionately attractive mates relative to their low sense of self-perceived mate value. In fact, incels appear acutely aware of their low mate value (Costello et al., 2023). The misogyny that pervades the incel community may be indicative of a low sense of self-perceived mate value among incels, as research shows that unwanted celibacy (independent of incel identity) is associated with misogynistic attitudes among men (Granau et al., 2022). Men are most inclined toward misogyny when they doubt their appeal to female partners (Bosson et al., 2022). Hostile sexism involves negative prejudices and stereotypes, while benevolent sexism reflects seemingly positive yet somewhat condescending beliefs about women (e.g., women need to be protected by men). There is evidence that women are attracted to benevolent sexism in a male romantic partner (Gul & Kupfer, 2019). Men who believe they are highly desirable to women tend to display both these hostile and benevolent forms of sexism consistently. However, men who see themselves as less desirable show more hostile rather than benevolent sexism. When low mate-value men doubt their abilities to protect and provide (needed for benevolent sexism), they may not embrace the benevolent sexism that can offset hostility and facilitate romantic attraction (Bosson et al., 2022; Gul & Kupfer, 2019).

Conclusions

Incels are a primarily online sub-culture community of men who forge a sense of identity around their perceived inability to form sexual or romantic relationships. The incel community operates almost exclusively online, providing an outlet to express misogynistic hostility, frustration, and blame toward society for a perceived failure to include them. Incels believe that genetic factors evolved mate preferences, and inequitable social structures restrict their access to sexual relationships with women. They believe that most women are attracted to a small number of men (Chads), who monopolize sexual encounters, while the "genetically inferior" incels are excluded from the gene pool.

Some research shows that incels are partially accurate about the socioeconomic conditions contributing to their plight. For example, incel activity is sensitive to the local mating ecology, and incels are more prevalent in geographic areas of: high-income inequality, low gender pay gaps, and male-biased sex ratios.

Foundational research has highlighted extremely poor mental health, some cognitive distortions, a victimhood mindset known, a disproportionate prevalence of autism spectrum disorder, poor mating intelligence, and dating anxiety among incels.

Historically, large groups of single young men have posed societal risks. However, the violent threat from incels appears limited. Some posit that digital spaces pacify potentially aggressive incels. More concerning, however, is their self-violence inclination, with numerous studies indicating their significant mental health struggles and suicidal tendencies. There is stronger evidence to suggest that incels are far more likely to be violent toward themselves than others, with several studies finding extremely poor levels of mental health and high levels of suicidality among this at-risk group.

Incel research is still in its infancy and must continue to grow. Although it is vital to conduct more human participant research with incels, it should be seen as complementary to both content and ecosystem analyses. Triangulating research from several different perspectives will offer us the best hopes of understanding the incel community. There is a particular need for intervention design and testing to help mitigate the problems incels face and represent in society.

References

Allely, C. S., Wilson, P., Minnis, H., Thompson, L., Yaksic, E., & Gillberg, C. (2017). Violence is rare in autism: When it does occur, is it sometimes extreme? *The Journal of Psychology, 151*(1), 49–68. https://doi.org/10.1080/00223980.2016.1175998

Andersen, J. C. (2023). The symbolic boundary work of incels: Subcultural negotiation of meaning and identity online. *Deviant Behavior, 44*(7), 1081–1101. https://doi.org/10.1080/01639625.2022.2142864

Apostolou, M., Shialos, M., & Georgiadou, P. (2019). The emotional cost of poor mating performance. *Personality and Individual Differences, 138*, 188–192. https://doi.org/10.1016/j.paid.2018.10.003

Apostolou, M., Sullman, M., Birkás, B., Błachnio, A., Bushina, E., Calvo, F., & Font-Mayolas, S. (2023). Mating performance and singlehood across 14 nations. *Evolutionary Psychology, 21*(1), 14747049221150168. https://doi.org/10.1177/14747049221150169

Baele, S., Brace, L., & Ging, D. (2023). A diachronic cross-platforms analysis of violent extremist language in the incel online ecosystem. *Terrorism and Political Violence*. https://doi.org/10.1080/09546553.2022.2161373

Baele, S. J., Brace, L., & Coan, T. G. (2021). From "Incel" to "Saint": Analyzing the violent worldview behind the 2018 Toronto attack. *Terrorism and Political Violence, 33*(8), 1667–1691. https://doi.org/10.1080/09546553.2019.1638256

Baron-Cohen, S. (1990). Autism: A specific cognitive disorder of & lsquo mind-blindness. *International Review of Psychiatry, 2*(1), 81–90. https://doi.org/10.3109/09540269009028274

Baselice, K. A. (2023). Analyzing Incels through the lens of evolutionary psychology. *Culture and Evolution*. https://doi.org/10.1556/2055.2022.00016

Bates, L. (2020). *The men who hate women: From incels to pickup artists, the truth about extreme misogyny and how it affects us all.* Simon and Schuster. https://www.simonandschuster.co.uk/books/Men-Who-Hate-Women/Laura-Bates/9781398504653

Baumeister, R. F., & Leary, M. R. (1995). The need to belong: Desire for interpersonal attachments as a fundamental human motivation. *Psychological Bulletin, 117*(3), 497. https://psycnet.apa.org/buy/1995-29052-001

Beauchamp, Z. (2019). Our Incel problem. Vox. Retrieved March 29, 2023, from https://www.vox.com/the-highlight/2019/4/16/18287446/incel-definition-reddit

Bendixen, M., & Kennair, L. E. O. (2017). When less is more: Psychometric properties of Norwegian short-forms of the Ambivalent Sexism Scales (ASI and AMI) and the Illinois Rape Myth Acceptance (IRMA) Scale. *Scandinavian Journal of Psychology, 58*(6), 541–550. https://doi.org/10.1111/sjop.12392

Ben Hamida, S., Mineka, S., & Bailey, J. M. (1998). Sex differences in perceived controllability of mate value: An evolutionary perspective. *Journal of Personality and Social Psychology, 75*(4), 953. https://doi.org/10.1037/0022-3514.75.4.953

Bjerkeset, O., Romundstad, P., & Gunnell, D. (2008). Gender differences in the association of mixed anxiety and depression with suicide. *The British Journal of Psychiatry, 192*(6), 474–475. https://doi.org/10.1192/bjp.bp.107.045203

Blake, K. R., & Brooks, R. C. (2022). Societies should not ignore their incel problem. *Trends in Cognitive Sciences*. https://doi.org/10.1016/j.tics.2022.11.007

Blake, K. R., O'Dean, S. M., Lian, J., & Denson, T. F. (2021). Misogynistic tweets correlate with violence against women. *Psychological Science, 32*(3), 315–325. https://doi.org/10.1177/0956797620968529

Bor, A., & Petersen, M. B. (2022). The psychology of online political hostility: A comprehensive, cross-national test of the mismatch hypothesis. *American Political Science Review, 116*(1), 1–18. https://doi.org/10.1017/S0003055421000885

Bosson, J. K., Rousis, G. J., & Felig, R. N. (2022). Curvilinear sexism and its links to men's perceived mate value. *Personality and Social Psychology Bulletin, 48*(4), 516–533. https://doi.org/10.1177/01461672211009726

Brace, L., Baele, S. J., & Ging, D. (2023). Where do 'mixed, unclear, and unstable' ideologies come from? A data-driven answer centred on the incelosphere. *Journal of Policing, Intelligence and Counter Terrorism, 1–22.* https://doi.org/10.1080/18335330.2023.2226667

Brody, S. (2010). The relative health benefits of different sexual activities. *The Journal of Sexual Medicine, 7*(4), 1336–1361. https://doi.org/10.1111/j.1743-6109.2009.01677.x

Brooks, R. C., Russo-Batterham, D., & Blake, K. R. (2022). Incel activity on social media linked to local mating ecology. *Psychological Science*, 09567976211036065.

Brzuszkiewicz, S. (2020). Incel radical milieu and external locus of control. *International Centre for Counter-Terrorism (ICCT).* https://doi.org/10.19165/2020.5.21

Buss, D. M. (2021). *Bad men: The hidden roots of sexual deception, harassment and assault*. Hachette UK.

Commission for Countering Extremism. (2021, February 24). *Operating with impunity: Hateful extremism—The need for a legal framework.* https://www.gov.uk/government/news/commission-for-countering-extremism-publishes-legal-review

Costello, W. (2023, May 23). The Allure of Inceldom: Why incels resist ascension. *Aporia Magazine*. Retrieved June 22, 2023, from https://www.aporiamagazine.com/p/the-allure-of-inceldom-why-incels

Costello, W., & Buss, D. M. (2023). Why isn't there more incel violence? *Adaptive Human Behavior and Physiology,* 1–8. https://doi.org/10.1007/s40750-023-00220-3

Costello, W., Rolon, V., Thomas, A. G., & Schmitt, D. (2022). Levels of well-being among men who are incel (involuntarily celibate). *Evolutionary Psychological Science*, *8*(4), 375–390. https://doi.org/10.1007/s40806-022-00336-x

Costello, W., Rolon, V., Thomas, A. G., & Schmitt, D. P. (2023). The mating psychology of incels (involuntary celibates): Misfortunes, misperceptions, and misrepresentations. *Journal of Sex Research,* 1–12. https://doi.org/10.1080/00224499.2023.2248096

Costello, W., Whittaker, J., & Thomas, A. G. (2025). The dual pathways hypothesis of incel harm: A model of harmful attitudes and beliefs among involuntary celibates. *Archives of Sexual Behavior*, 1–22. https://doi.org/10.1007/s10508-025-03161-y

Cottee, S. (2020). Incel (E) motives: Resentment, shame and revenge. *Studies in Conflict & Terrorism, 44*(2), 93–114. https://doi.org/10.1080/1057610X.2020.1822589

Crimando, S. (2019). Alone together and angry: An Incel revolution. *Security Management, 63*(3), 32–37.

Daly, S. E., & Laskovtsov, A. (2021). "Goodbye, my friendcels": An analysis of incel suicide posts. *CrimRxiv*. https://doi.org/10.21428/cb6ab371.a9564fcd

Daly, S. E., & Nichols, A. L. (2023). 'Incels are shit-post kings': Incels' perceptions of online forum content. *Journal of Crime and Justice*, 1–23. https://doi.org/10.1080/0735648X.2023.2169330

Daly, S. E., & Reed, S. M. (2022). "I think most of society hates us": A qualitative thematic analysis of interviews with incels. *Sex Roles, 86*(1–2), 14–33. https://doi.org/10.1007/s11199-021-01250-5

Diamond, M. (1999). The effects of pornography: An international perspective. In J. Elias et al. (Eds.), *Pornography 101: Eroticism, sexuality, and the first amendment*. Prometheus Press.

Diamond, M., Jozifkova, E., & Weiss, P. (2011). Pornography and sex crimes in the Czech Republic. *Archives of Sexual Behavior, 40*, 1037–1043. https://doi.org/10.1007/s10508-0109696-y

Donnelly, D., Burgess, E., Anderson, S., Davis, R., & Dillard, J. (2001). Involuntary celibacy: A life course analysis. *Journal of Sex Research, 38*(2), 159–169. https://doi.org/10.1080/00224490109552083

de Catanzaro, D. (1995). Reproductive status, family interactions, and suicidal ideation: Surveys of the general public and high-risk groups. *Ethology and Sociobiology, 16*(5), 385–394. https://doi.org/10.1016/0162-3095(95)00055-0

Edlund, L., Yi, J., Li, H., & Zhang, J. (2013). Sex ratios and crime: Evidence from China. *The Review of Economics and Statistics, 95*, 1520–1534. https://doi.org/10.1162/REST_a_00356

Ellenberg, M., Speckhard, A., & Kruglanski, A. W. (2023). Beyond violent extremism: A 3N perspective of inceldom. *Psychology of Men & Masculinities*. https://doi.org/10.1037/men0000439

Elsabbagh, M., Divan, G., Koh, Y. J., Kim, Y. S., Kauchali, S., Marcín, C., & Fombonne, E. (2012). Global prevalence of autism and other pervasive developmental disorders. *Autism Research, 5*(3), 160–179. https://doi.org/10.1002/aur.239

Fleischman, D. (2020, October 30). Uncanny vulvas. Dianaverse. https://dianaverse.com/2020/10/30/uncanny-vulvas/

Gabay, R., Hameiri, B., Rubel-Lifschitz, T., & Nadler, A. (2020). The tendency for interpersonal victimhood: The personality construct and its consequences.

Personality and Individual Differences, 165, Article 110134. https://doi.org/10.1016/j.paid.2020.110134

Geher, G., Kaufman, S. B., Garcia, J. R., Kaufman, J. C., & Dawson, B. B. (2016). The validity and structure of mating intelligence. *Evolution, Mind and Behaviour, 14*(1), 1–22. https://doi.org/10.1556/2050.2016.0001

Gilbert, P. (1998). The evolved basis and adaptive functions of cognitive distortions. *British Journal of Medical Psychology, 71*(4), 447–463. https://doi.org/10.1111/j.2044-8341.1998.tb01002.x

Glace, A. M., Dover, T. L., & Zatkin, J. G. (2021). Taking the black pill: An empirical analysis of the "Incel." *Psychology of Men & Masculinities*. https://doi.org/10.1037/men0000328

Glick, P., & Fiske, S. T. (2018). The ambivalent sexism inventory: Differentiating hostile and benevolent sexism. In *Social cognition* (pp. 116–160). Routledge. https://www.taylorfrancis.com/chapters/edit/10.4324/9781315187280-6/ambivalent-sexism-inventory-peter-glick-susan-fiske

Goetz, C. D., Pillsworth, E. G., Buss, D. M., & Conroy-Beam, D. (2019). Evolutionary mismatch in mating. *Frontiers in Psychology, 10*, 2709. https://doi.org/10.3389/fpsyg.2019.02709

Gothard, K. C. (2020). Exploring incel language and subreddit activity on reddit. *UVM Honors College Senior Theses*, 408. https://scholarworks.uvm.edu/hcoltheses/408

Grunau, K., Bieselt, H. E., Gul, P., & Kupfer, T. R. (2022). Unwanted celibacy is associated with misogynistic attitudes even after controlling for personality. *Personality and Individual Differences, 199*, Article 111860. https://doi.org/10.1016/j.paid.2022.111860

Gul, P., & Kupfer, T. R. (2019). Benevolent sexism and mate preferences: Why do women prefer benevolent men despite recognizing that they can be undermining? *Personality and Social Psychology Bulletin, 45*(1), 146–161. https://doi.org/10.1177/0146167218781000

Guttentag, M., & Secord, P. F. (1983). *Too many women? The sex ratio question*. Sage.

Hagen, E. H. (2003). The bargaining model of depression. In *Genetic and cultural evolution of cooperation* (pp. 95–123).

Hahnel-Peeters, R. K., Goetz, A. T., & Goetz, C. D. (2022). Do environmental cues to discovery influence the likelihood to rape? *Evolutionary Psychology, 20*(4), 14747049221141078. https://doi.org/10.1177/14747049221141078

Hall, J. (2023). *The terrorism acts in 2021*. The Stationary Office.

Halpin, M., Richard, N., Preston, K., Gosse, M., & Maguire, F. (2023). Men who hate women: The misogyny of involuntarily celibate men. *New Media & Society*, 14614448231176776. https://doi.org/10.1177/14614448231176777

Hamilton, F. (2021, September 29). Plymouth shooting: Jake Davison attack wasn't 'incel' terrorism, says officer. *The Times*. https://www.thetimes.co.uk/article/plymouth-shooting-jake-davison-attack-wasnt-incel-terrorism-says-officer-sc2mzx9q3

Harper, C. R., Dittus, P. J., Leichliter, J. S., & Aral, S. O. (2017). Changes in the distribution of sex partners in the United States: 2002 to 2011–2013. *Sexually Transmitted Diseases, 44*(2), 96–100. https://doi.org/10.1097/OLQ.0000000000000554

Hart, G., & Huber, A. R. (2023). Five things we need to learn about incel extremism: Issues, challenges and avenues for fresh research. *Studies in Conflict & Terrorism*, 1–17. https://doi.org/10.1080/1057610X.2023.2195067

Hinds, Z. (2022). *True or false incels: An analysis of the Incels.is forum* (Thesis). University of Chicago. https://doi.org/10.6082/uchicago.4217

Hoffman, B., Ware, J., & Shapiro, E. (2020). Assessing the threat of incel violence. *Studies in Conflict & Terrorism, 43*(7), 565–587. https://doi.org/10.1080/1057610X.2020.1751459

Holt-Lunstad, J., Smith, T. B., Baker, M., Harris, T., & Stephenson, D. (2015). Loneliness and social isolation as risk factors for mortality: A meta-analytic review. *Perspectives on Psychological Science, 10*(2), 227–237. https://doi.org/10.1177/1745691614568352

Home Office. (2023). *Individuals referred to and supported through the Prevent Programme, April 2021 to March 2022*. https://www.gov.uk/government/statistics/individuals-referred-to-and-supported-through-the-prevent-programme-april-2021-to-march-2022/individuals-referred-to-and-supported-through-the-prevent-programme-april-2021-to-march-2022

H.M. Government. (2020). Channel duty guidance protecting vulnerable people from being drawn into terrorism.

Incels.co. (2020, March). *Survey results—March 2020*. https://incels.co/threads/survey-results-march-2020.188748/page-3

Institute for Research on Male Supremacism. (n.d.). Recommendations for media reporting on incels. https://theirms.org/forjournalists

Jaki, S., De Smedt, T., Gwóźdź, M., Panchal, R., Rossa, A., & De Pauw, G. (2019). Online hatred of women in the Incels.me forum: Linguistic analysis and automatic detection. *Journal of Language Aggression and Conflict*, *7*(2), 240–268. https://doi.org/10.1075/jlac.00026.jak

Kenrick, D. T., Neuberg, S. L., Griskevicius, V., Becker, D. V., & Schaller, M. (2010). Goal-driven cognition and functional behavior. *Current Directions in Psychological Science, 19*(1), 63–67. https://doi.org/10.1177/0963721409359281

Kiss, A. (2022). Incels: Frustrated and angry due to deprivation of intimacy: A case study of the radicalisation trajectories of an online community on a fringe social media platform. https://www.diva-portal.org/smash/record.jsf?pid=diva2%3A1673271&dswid=4061

Kirsner, B. R., Figueredo, A. J., & Jacobs, W. J. (2003). Self, friends, and lovers: Structural relations among Beck Depression Inventory scores and perceived mate values. *Journal of Affective Disorders, 75*(2), 131–148.

Kowert, R., Martel, A., & Swann, W. B. (2022). Not just a game: Identity fusion and extremism in gaming cultures. *Frontiers in Communication,* 226. https://doi.org/10.3389/fcomm.2022.1007128

Krahn, H., Hatnagel, T. F., & Gartrell, J. W. (1986). Income inequality and homicide rates: Cross-national data and criminological theories. *Criminology, 24*(2), 269–294. https://doi.org/10.1111/j.1745-9125.1986.tb01496.x

Kugeares, S. L. (2002). *Social anxiety in dating initiation: An experimental investigation of an evolved mating-specific anxiety mechanism* (Order No. 3110639). Dissertations & Theses @ University of Texas—Austin; ProQuest Dissertations & Theses Global. (305512408).

Kutchinsky, B. (1973). The effect of easy availability of pornography on the incidence of sex crimes: The Danish experience. *Journal of Social Issues, 29*(3), 163–181. https://doi.org/10.1111/j.1540-4560.1973.tb00094.x

Kutchinsky, B. (1991). Pornography and rape: Theory and practice? Evidence from crime data in four countries where pornography is easily available. *International Journal of Law and Psychiatry, 14*(1–2), 47–64. https://doi.org/10.1016/0160-2527(91)90024-H

Kutchinsky, S. (2019). I used to be an incel. *BBC*. https://www.bbc.co.uk/bbcthree/article/45bdcd7a-1cb1-4ad1-a3e0-ebc2a05243ac.

Lankford, A. (2021). A sexual frustration theory of aggression, violence, and crime. *Journal of Criminal Justice, 77*, Article 101865. https://doi.org/10.1016/j.jcrimjus.2021.101865

Li, N. P., Yong, J. C., Tsai, M. H., Lai, M. H., Lim, A. J., & Ackerman, J. M. (2020). Confidence is sexy and it can be trained: Examining male social confidence in initial, opposite-sex interactions. *Journal of Personality, 88*(6), 1235–1251. https://doi.org/10.1111/jopy.12568

Lindsay, A. (2022). Swallowing the black pill: Involuntary celibates' (Incels) anti-feminism within digital society. *International Journal for Crime, Justice and Social Democracy, 11*(1), 210–224.

Malamuth, N. M. (1981). Rape proclivity among males. *Journal of Social Issues, 37*(4), 138–157. https://doi.org/10.1111/j.1540-4560.1981.tb01075.x

Minassian, R. V. (2021). ONSC 1258 (Ont. S.C.J. Mar. 3, 2021). https://www.courthousenews.com/wp-content/uploads/2021/03/Queen_Minassian-VERDICT

Moskalenko, S., González, J. F. G., Kates, N., & Morton, J. (2022). Incel ideology, radicalization and mental health: A survey study. *The Journal of*

Intelligence, Conflict, and Warfare, 4(3), 1–29. https://doi.org/10.21810/jicw.v4i3.3817

Ok, E., Qian, Y., Strejcek, B., & Aquino, K. (2021). Signaling virtuous victimhood as indicators of Dark Triad personalities. *Journal of Personality and Social Psychology, 120*(6), 1634. https://doi.org/10.1037/pspp0000329

Palmer, J. E., McMahon, S., & Fissel, E. (2021). Correlates of incoming male college students' proclivity to perpetrate sexual assault. *Violence against Women, 27*(3–4), 507–528. https://doi.org/10.1177/1077801220905663

Pelzer, B., Kaati, L., Cohen, K., & Fernquist, J. (2021). Toxic language in online incel communities. *SN Social Sciences, 1*(8), 1–22. https://doi.org/10.1007/s43545-021-00220-8

Pennebaker, J. W., Francis, M. E., & Booth, R. J. (2001). Linguistic inquiry and word count: LIWC 2001. *Mahway: Lawrence Erlbaum Associates, 71*(2001).

Perliger, A., Stevens, C., & Leidig, E. (2023). *Mapping the ideological landscape of extreme misogyny. ICCT Research Paper*.

Pietromonaco, P. R., & Beck, L. A. (2019). Adult attachment and physical health. *Current Opinion in Psychology, 25*, 115–120. https://doi.org/10.1016/j.copsyc.2018.04.004

Pinker, S. (2018). *Enlightenment now: The case for reason, science, humanism, and progress*. Penguin.

Płatos, M., Wojaczek, K., & Laugeson, E. A. (2023). Fostering friendship and dating skills among adults on the autism spectrum: A randomized controlled trial of the polish version of the PEERS® for young adults curriculum. *Journal of Autism and Developmental Disorders,* 1–16. https://doi.org/10.1007/s10803-023-05921-y

Raque-Bogdan, T. L., Ericson, S. K., Jackson, J., Martin, H. M., & Bryan, N. A. (2011). Attachment and mental and physical health: Self-compassion and mattering as mediators. *Journal of Counselling Psychology, 58*(2), 272. https://doi.org/10.1037/a0023041

Räsänen, J. (2023). Sexual loneliness: A neglected public health problem? *Bioethics, 37*(2), 101–102. https://doi.org/10.1111/bioe.13134

Reuters. (2023, March 9). Islamist militants kill at least 25 in Nigeria's Borno state. *Reuters*. Retrieved June 22, 2023, from https://www.reuters.com/world/africa/islamist-militants-kill-least-25-nigerias-borno-state-2023-03-09/

Ribeiro, M. H., Blackburn, J., Bradlyn, B., De Cristofaro, E., Stringhini, G., Long, S., Greenberg, S., & Zannettou, S. (2021, May). The evolution of the manosphere across the web. In *Proceedings of the international AAAI conference on web and social media* (Vol. 15, pp. 196–207). https://doi.org/10.1609/icwsm.v15i1.18053

Rodger, E. (2014). My twisted world: The story of Elliot Rodger. Retrieved February, 3, 2016.

Rousis, J., Martel, A. F., Bosson, J. K., & Swann, W. B. (2023). Behind the blackpill: Self-verification and identity fusion predict endorsement of violence against women among self-identified incels. *Personality and Social Psychology Bulletin*. https://doi.org/10.1177/01461672231166481

Shawcross, W. (2023, February 8). *Independent review of prevent's report and government response*. https://www.gov.uk/government/publications/independent-review-of-prevents-report-and-government-response; https://doi.org/10.1007/s11920-022-01382-9

Sparks, B., Zidenberg, A. M., & Olver, M. E. (2022). Involuntary celibacy: A review of incel ideology and experiences with dating, rejection, and associated mental health and emotional sequelae. *Current Psychiatry Reports*, 1–10. https://doi.org/10.1007/s11920-022-01382-9

Sparks, B., Zidenberg, A. M., & Olver, M. E. (2023). One is the loneliest number: Involuntary celibacy (incel), mental health, and loneliness. *Current Psychology*, 1–15. https://doi.org/10.1007/s12144-023-04275-z

Speckhard, A., & Ellenberg, M. (2022). Self-reported psychiatric disorder and perceived psychological symptom rates among involuntary celibates (incels) and their perceptions of mental health treatment. *Behavioral Sciences of Terrorism and Political Aggression*, 1–18. https://doi.org/10.1080/19434472.2022.2029933

Speckhard, A., Ellenberg, M., Morton, J., & Ash, A. (2021). Involuntary celibates' experiences of and grievance over sexual exclusion and the potential threat of violence among those active in an online incel forum. *Journal of Strategic Security*, *14*(2), 5. https://doi.org/10.5038/1944-0472.14.2.1910

Srinivasan, A. (2021). *The right to sex*. Bloomsbury Publishing.

Stijelja, S., & Mishara, B. L. (2022). Psychosocial characteristics of involuntary celibates (Incels): A review of empirical research and assessment of the potential implications of research on adult virginity and late sexual onset. *Sexuality & Culture*, 1–20. https://doi.org/10.1007/s12119-022-10031-5

Sunstein, C. R. (1999). The law of group polarization. *University of Chicago Law School, John M. Olin Law & Economics Working Paper*, 91.

Swann, W. B., Pelham, B. W., & Chidester, T. R. (1988). Change through paradox: Using self-verification to alter beliefs. *Journal of Personality and Social Psychology*, *54*(2), 268. https://doi.org/10.1037/0022-3514.54.2.268

Thomas, M. F., Binder, A., & Matthes, J. (2022). The agony of partner choice: The effect of excessive partner availability on fear of being single, self-esteem, and partner choice overload. *Computers in Human Behavior*, *126*, Article 106977. https://doi.org/10.1016/j.chb.2021.106977

Tooby, J., & Cosmides, L. (1990). The past explains the present: Emotional adaptations and the structure of ancestral environments. *Ethology and Sociobiology*, *11*(4–5), 375–424. https://doi.org/10.1016/0162-3095(90)90017-Z

Van de Velde, S., Bracke, P., & Levecque, K. (2010). Gender differences in depression in 23 European countries. Cross-national variation in the gender gap in depression. *Social science & Medicine*, *71*(2), 305–313. https://doi.org/10.1016/j.socscimed.2010.03.035

Wachowski, A., Wachowski, L., Reeves, K., Fishburne, L., Moss, C. A., Weaving, H., & Staenberg, Z. (1999). *The Matrix*. Warner Home Video.

Wilson, M., & Daly, M. (1985). Competitiveness, risk taking, and violence: The young male syndrome. *Ethology and Sociobiology*, *6*(1), 59–73. https://doi.org/10.1016/0162-3095(85)90041-X

Wintemute, G. J., Robinson, S., Crawford, A., Schleimer, J. P., Barnhorst, A., Chaplin, V., & Pear, V. A. (2022). Views of American democracy and society and support for political violence: First report from a nationwide population-representative survey. *medRxiv*, 2022-07. https://doi.org/10.1101/2022.07.15.22277693.

Young, R. K., & Thiessen, D. (1992). The Texas rape scale. *Ethology and Sociobiology*, *13*(1), 19–33. https://doi.org/10.1016/0162-3095(92)90004-N

Zdjelar, V. (2020). *Alone together: Exploring community on an incel forum* (Doctoral dissertation, Simon Fraser University). http://summit.sfu.ca/item/21191.

Glossary

Autism spectrum disorder (ASD) and incels: A noted prevalence of ASD among self-identified incels, potentially contributing to difficulties in social interaction and dating.

Benevolent sexism: A seemingly positive but patronizing form of sexism that casts women as needing protection and support from men.

Beta (Normie): A term used in the incel community to describe average-looking men who are perceived as neither particularly successful nor particularly unsuccessful in the mating market.

Blackmail: Using threats (usually of exposure of secret/incriminating documents, media, or information) to make another person conform to your demands.

Black pill: A pessimistic worldview held by many incels, which asserts that their romantic and sexual circumstances are unchangeable due to genetic determinism and social inequities.

Chad: A term used by incels to describe an attractive, high-status man who is perceived as monopolizing sexual access to women.

Child sexual exploitation/abuse Material: Sexually explicit images or videos of children. This sometimes includes images or videos of the children being physically and sexually abused.

Coercive techniques: Tactics and behaviours (including threats and force) used to compel someone to perform actions against their will.

Cyberflashing: A form of sexual harassment or abuse that falls under the umbrella of image-based sexual abuse wherein an individual sends

C. A. Harper et al. (eds.), *Sexual Crime and the Internet*, Sexual Crime,
https://doi.org/10.1007/978-3-031-95844-1

unsolicited sexual images or videos to an unsuspecting person. It is a gender-neutral term in comparison to the colloquial expression "dick pic," which referred to the practice of men sending sexual material of their genitals, primarily to women.

Dark triad: A collection of personality traits including psychopathy, narcissism, and Machiavellianism.

Dating anxiety: Extreme nervousness or fear associated with romantic or sexual interactions, commonly reported among incels.

Deepfaking: The use of artificial intelligence and machine learning technology to merge the likeness of one person onto a secondary stimulus, such as an image or video.

Hostile sexism: A form of sexism characterized by antagonistic attitudes toward women, including beliefs that women manipulate men for personal gain.

Identity fusion: A psychological phenomenon in which an individual strongly merges their sense of self with a group identity, often linked to extreme beliefs or behaviours.

Image-based sexual abuse (IBSA): A category of technology-facilitated sexual violence that focuses on image- and video-based acts. This includes the creation and/or distribution of intimate or sexual images without a person's consent or the threat to distribute sexual media of a person without their consent.

Incels (involuntary celibates): A primarily online subculture of men who self-identify as being unable to form sexual or romantic relationships despite wanting to.

Incel suicide risk: The elevated rates of depression and suicidality observed among incels, likely linked to loneliness and lack of romantic success.

Interpersonal victimhood (TIV): A psychological construct describing an enduring sense of victimization, often linked to resentment and social grievances.

Male sedation hypothesis: A speculative theory suggesting that online activities such as pornography and video games pacify sexless men who might otherwise engage in aggressive behaviour.

Mate deprivation hypothesis: A controversial theory suggesting that lack of sexual access increases the likelihood of men engaging in sexually coercive behaviours.

Mating intelligence: A set of cognitive and social abilities related to navigating the mating market successfully, including the ability to accurately perceive mate preferences.

Online misogyny: Hatred, hostility, or discrimination toward women expressed in digital spaces, often amplified in incel forums.

Online radicalization: The process by which individuals adopt extreme beliefs through online communities and digital echo chambers.

Proclivity: A propensity for, or self-reported willingness to engage in, a particular behaviour.

Psychoeducation: A form of mental health intervention that focuses on learning about a particular mental health concept or process, and therefore developing an understanding of it, which is thought to aid somebody to cope with and seek support for their difficulties.

Rejection sensitivity: Heightened emotional reactivity to perceived social rejection, which may contribute to incels' negative self-perceptions.

Revenge pornography: A colloquial term used to describe the non-consensual sharing of private sexual images of another person.

Self-verification theory: The psychological tendency for individuals to seek confirmation of their self-views, even if those views are negative.

Sexting: The sending of sexual messages and/or audiovisual materials to a consenting party, often a current or prospective romantic or sexual partner.

Sextortion: Using coercive tactics or blackmail to force a victim to engage in sexual activities, or provide sexually explicit images/video.

Sexual frustration theory of aggression: The idea that sexual deprivation can contribute to aggression, though empirical evidence is mixed.

Sexual selection: An evolutionary process by which individuals with traits that enhance reproductive success are more likely to pass on their genes.

Stacy: A term used by incels to describe an attractive, high-status woman who is perceived as only dating Chads.

Technology-facilitated sexual violence (TFSV): A term used to capture sexually aggressive or violent behaviours (or threat of behaviours) that are enabled or furthered by technology. Namely, this refers to the expression of sexual aggression using digital communications, such as coercing someone to engage in sexting, sharing intimate images of a person to a third party without consent, or using online communication services to sexually harass a person.

Upskirting: The act of stealthily taking a picture of somebody's genitals or buttocks underneath their clothes.

Young male syndrome: An evolutionary psychology concept describing the tendency of unpartnered young men to engage in risk-taking and aggressive behaviours to gain social status and attract mates.

Index

C. A. Harper et al. (eds.), *Sexual Crime and the Internet*, Sexual Crime, https://doi.org/10.1007/978-3-031-95844-1

The manufacturer's authorised representative in the EU is Springer Nature Customer Service Centre GmbH, Europaplatz 3, 69115 Heidelberg, Germany. If you have any concerns regarding our products, please contact ProductSafety@springernature.com

Printed and bound by CPI Group (UK) Ltd, Croydon, CR0 4YY
05/10/2026
02228155-0005